ELEANOR ROOSEVELT

LIVES TO REMEMBER

Eleanor Roosevelt

by Alfred Steinberg

ILLUSTRATED BY ANDRÉ LE BLANC

G. P. PUTNAM'S SONS
NEW YORK

For Arne, Lise and Polly

CONTENTS

ELEANOR ROOSEVELT

LIVES TO REMEMBER

Chapter 1

UNCLE TED'S SWAN

THE carriage clattered up the long, arched driveway to the big house on Sagamore Hill in Oyster Bay. "Hyer! Hyer!" the driver called, as the frisky dogs yelped at the hoofs of the horses. The children on the porch and lawn stopped their games to watch the arrival.

From the back seat of the bumping vehicle, ten-year-old Eleanor Roosevelt took in the happy scene. An orphan and sad, her clear blue eyes sought eagerly for carefree joy. A weekend with Uncle Ted and her Cousin Roosevelts—what could be more exciting? She almost gasped aloud. Nervously, she fluffed her silky, brown hair and tugged at the hem of her skimpy, hand-me-down dress in a vain effort to pull it below her knees.

Then the carriage was at the porch and Uncle Ted came flying down the stairs to catch her in his arms. "Darling, darling Eleanor." He squeezed her in a bear hug that tore all the gathers out of her frock. "Bully! I'm so glad you've come." He thrust out a big fist and shook it up and down with delight.

This was her father's older brother and close companion of his childhood. Three years later Uncle Ted would be leading the Rough Riders in their charge up San Juan Hill in the Spanish-American War of 1898. Three short years after that he would be President of the United States.

It was a weekend the tall, shy girl would never forget. For two days she did not have time to think about her lone-

9

liness, nor about her dead mother, father and little brother "Ellie."

Uncle Ted started things off by taking a dozen children swimming. Those who lingered on the dock he threw into the water. When Eleanor saw him coming, she screamed and jumped into the water. She came up sputtering and Uncle Ted grinned. Later they played "Follow The Leader," with Uncle Ted in the lead and all the children lined up behind him and holding hands, as he pulled them headlong down Cooper's Bluff into the water. They rolled most of the way down for the bluff was steep. Then he chased them through the grounds, into the barn and up into the hayloft.

At dinnertime he took them to a place on the shore where Eleanor joined the others in cooking supper. When the food was gone, Uncle Ted pulled a book from a pocket and read aloud. Everyone sat hushed because he read so well, and was an author besides. Then when it rained, he raced them to the gun room on the top floor of the house. There were buffalo, deer and elk that he had shot out West, and their stuffed heads were on the walls. Once the children were quiet again and the kerosene lamps were lit, he told them tales of adventure and bravery and humorous little stories that he made up as he went along.

It was all over too soon for Eleanor. Uncle Ted was helping her into the carriage for the return ride to Grandmother Hall's place at Tivoli-on-Hudson. There were tears of joy and regret in her eyes, while his eyes wore a sad expression. "This is no way for the Police Commissioner of New York to act," he chuckled. "We had a bully time, Eleanor, didn't we?" He kissed her cheek.

"Yes," she cried in a high voice, as the carriage horses trotted off. She waved at Uncle Ted, Aunt Eleanor and all the children long after they were out of sight.

After Eleanor was gone, Uncle Ted's wife sat down to write a letter to Eleanor's Auntie Bye in London. Her heart had ached at the sight of the lonely child. Yet her pen poured out a prophesy. "Poor little soul," she wrote Bye about Eleanor. "She is very plain. Her mouth and teeth seem to have no future, but the ugly duckling may turn out to be a swan."

Chapter 2

GRANNY AND LITTLE NELL

ELEANOR ROOSEVELT was born in New York City on October 11, 1884. By birth, she was a member of two of the best-regarded New York families. On her mother's side she was a direct descendant of Chancelor Livingston, who administered the oath of office to George Washington when he became President in 1789. Her father's first American ancestor was a Dutch peasant, Claes Martenszen of the Rosefield, who came to New Amsterdam in the 1640's. Claes's son Nicholas, who legally took on the family name of Roosevelt, began the Roosevelt tradition of wealth and interest in the outdoors. There were also adventurers in Eleanor's background. Great-uncle James Bullock was the agent for the Confederate Government in England during the Civil War. It was Uncle Jimmy who built the *Alabama,* the Confederate privateer that sank so many Union ships.

Eleanor's father, Elliott Roosevelt, two years younger than his brother Theodore, was a handsome young man with a passion for hunting. He hunted wild game in Africa and India and was known as one of the best shots in the Wild West when he and brother Ted hunted together across the Mississippi. He was a tall, muscular man with a thick mustache and eyes full of kindness.

Eleanor's mother, Anna, was the daughter of Valentine and Mary Livingston Hall of Tivoli-on-Hudson, New York. New York social leaders called her the most beautiful woman in New York City. She had a great desire to become an actress, but her family background as well as her religious training kept her from this. She was a proud and self-reliant young woman who had had to take over the management of her family while in her teens when her father died in 1880.

With money enough to do as she wished and blessed with beauty and wide interests, Anna Roosevelt was nevertheless unhappy. She had expected her daughter to look like the Halls and Livingstons. Instead, by the time little Eleanor was able to crawl, she saw that Eleanor favored the Roosevelts. Especially did she resemble her husband's brother Ted, with her straight brows, eyelids drooping at the corners and large mouth and teeth. "Granny," she called little Eleanor when she started to walk, and wondered why her daughter never smiled.

Once when Eleanor was two years old, she went with her parents to visit another branch of her father's family, the Roosevelts of Hyde Park. The four-year-old heir in that house was Franklin Delano Roosevelt, who was the godson of Eleanor's father. Franklin carried her on his back in the nursery, as if he were a bucking bronco. Afterward when Eleanor stood in the doorway of the living room, her mother called out, "Come in, Granny." Then turning to her host and hostess, James and Sara Delano Roosevelt, she explained, "She is such a funny child, so old-fashioned that we always call her Granny." Young as she was, Eleanor felt a great pain in her heart.

There was nothing she could do to change her mother's opinion of her. The disappointment in her appearance led to general fault-finding. "I was always disgracing my mother," said Eleanor.

If Eleanor was forever uneasy with her mother, she was always joyous with her father. Each morning she rushed to his dressing room and he would hold her high in the air while he spun her about. Sometimes when her parents had

company he would ask her to dance and she would whirl
about the room, and then hurry into his waiting arms afterward for a kiss. "Little Nell," he called her, after the sweet
little heroine in Charles Dickens' *Old Curiosity Shop.*

Her mother complained that she would dirty her dress a
minute after putting it on. On the other hand, her father
wanted her to be a tomboy and love the outdoors, without
paying constant attention to her clothes. Once he wrote to
his sister Bye with pride: "Little Eleanor is as happy as the
day is long, plays with her kitten, the puppies and the
chickens all the time, and is very dirty as a general rule."

Though her mother impressed upon her the opinion
that she was not very bright, her father considered her to
be intelligent far beyond her years. Often he read to her.
Even though she could not read, at four she listened to him
closely and memorized a large part of "Hiawatha." Then
she recited it back to him, while he stared proudly into her
eyes.

He meant excitement to her. There was danger everywhere and he was the master who would keep her safe.
Sometimes he took her riding. He had a splendid, sleek
horse named Mohawk that pulled an open carriage as if he
were in a championship race. Once Eleanor's father took
her for a ride through Central Park, where he warned her
that Mohawk would jump over all the other carts in the
road if he shouted "Hoopla!"

"Oh, Papa!" she told him, her heart pounding. "I hope
you won't say it!"

His eyes twinkled. "I won't if you don't want me to."

He was, of course, her hero, too, in the real meaning of
the word. When she was four, she started out to Europe by
steamer with her parents. A heavy fog developed soon after
they left New York Harbor. The captain tooted his fog-
horn repeatedly. But despite this caution, another ship
rammed into theirs. Wild confusion followed. Passengers

shoved and pushed and Eleanor was separated from her parents.

Suddenly she found herself leaning terrifiedly over the railing. Far down below she spied her father standing in a little boat and holding up his arms to her. "Jump!" he yelled. She shrieked, then jumped and he caught her. "There, there, Little Nell," he comforted her. "Everything is all right now."

So she was "Granny" to her mother and "Little Nell" to her father, a situation that made her unhappy and happy at the same time. Within herself she dreamed that someday she would do something that would win her mother's favor. Then her life would be completely joyous.

So the troubled first few years passed. . . .

The routine of her life changed swiftly by a single incident. Her father was a gifted horseman and when he promised to ride a spirited horse in a society circus, her mother was proud. He had been going into town each day to his business office, and it was some time since he had been on a horse.

With a fast-beating heart, Eleanor watched her father leave the house that day. But he was back in a few hours, being carried into his room and groaning all the while. To her horror, she learned that he had been thrown from the horse and his leg broken. "I was dissolved in tears and sobbed my heart out for hours," she said.

He never really recovered from that accident. The leg was not set properly and had to be rebroken and reset. In the winter of 1890, shortly after the birth of her brother Elliott, Eleanor went to Europe with her parents. For a short time her father seemed better. In Venice, he took her out on the canals and acted as gondolier, singing louder if not better than the Italian boatmen. At Vesuvius, they threw pennies into the lava.

Once Papa was especially proud of her and called her a

real Roosevelt. At Sorrento, Italy, she went for a ride over
the steep hills on a donkey with a donkey-boy guide leading
the way. However, when they returned, the boy sat astride
the donkey while she ran alongside. "But Papa," she cried,
"he was barefoot and his feet were bleeding." Her father
beamed and held her close.

But her fun with her father was short-lived. When he
took a turn for the worse, he entered a sanitarium in Ger-

many. Her mother and baby Ellie went to live in a house outside of Paris. Eleanor, not yet six, was sent to a convent. "You are not pretty," her mother warned her before her departure, "so see to it that your manners compensate for your looks."

She was alone now and bewildered in a strange country. The little girls in the convent ignored her because she could not speak French. Daily she wandered in the walled-in garden and worried about her father. Would he ever be well again and twirl her about in his arms?

Once when she wanted attention from the other girls, she told one of the nuns that she had swallowed a penny. It had seemed like a harmless lie to her. But the sisters of the convent sent for her mother and told her they did not want a liar in their midst. Her mother felt completely disgraced and scolded her all the way back to Paris. She not only had no looks but her manners were worse. What would she possibly turn into when she grew up?

They were back in New York now—that is, everyone but her father. Another brother, Gracie Hall, was born shortly before they left France. Mama was especially close with Ellie and Hall, and Eleanor felt a barrier between herself and the three. Nevertheless, she tried in many ways to win her mother's favor. For instance, when her mother's worries regarding her father brought on painful headaches, Eleanor often sat at the head of her bed and stroked her head for hours at a time. In return, her mother let her sleep in her bedroom, though she forbade her to use sugar on her food and made her recite on awakening a memorized verse from the Old or the New Testament.

Word came to Eleanor that Uncle Ted had gone to Europe and brought her father home. But he hadn't brought him to her. Instead, he had taken him to Abingdon, Virginia, where her father was to live, she was told, until he had recovered. Fortunately, a great-aunt had dis-

overed when Eleanor was six that she had never been to
chool and could not read or write. A summer of hard
vork had taught her the simple words of English. So now
he could write to her father, though her mother frowned
at her poor spelling.

In the fall of 1892, a diptheria epidemic hit New York.
Doctors came hurriedly to the house and stayed all night
when her mother fell ill. A telegram went out to her father
to come at once. A freak snowstorm had made the train late
and he stood on the tracks, he later told Eleanor, to flag it
down. But he arrived too late. By the time he burst through
the doorway, her mother was dead.

Eleanor had never seen her father so sad. In many ways
she tried to ease his burden. An aunt reminded her later:
"Just after your mother's death, when he was in such
sorrow, he wrote of his 'little Nell' being the greatest help
and comfort to him with her loving sympathy and again,
that same period, he wrote of going to church with you
and of your 'nestling close to Father' and looking over the
same prayer book with him."

It was arranged that Eleanor and her two younger broth-
ers were to live with Grandmother Hall in her sprawling
place outside of Tivoli up the Hudson. "Some day," her
father told her before he left for Abingdon, "we will live
together again and you will make a home for me. You and
I will travel together and have fun the way we used to.
Now write often, be a good girl, don't give any trouble,
study hard and grow up into a woman I can be proud of."
She promised him tearfully and he kissed her good-by.

Another tragedy brought them together again soon after
her mother's death. Ellie and Hall came down with scarlet
fever. Ellie, who was only four, also caught diptheria. For
days he lingered with a high fever and then he died.

After this, Eleanor's father seemed older. He began writing her many letters from Abingdon and occasionally he

came to New York to take her riding in the park and to dinner. "You and I must keep close together," he repeated. Somehow, even when he did not tell her in advance that he was coming, she sensed that he was on his way. At least a dozen times she rushed from her room and slid down the banister in time to greet him, even though his visit was a surprise.

He had a feeling that his little daughter would amount to something in life, and he told her so. He wrote her several letters full of morals to guide her on that road. He told her how important it was to have goals in life, good working and living habits, and sympathy for others. From Abingdon, several girls wrote her that her father had given them dolls and they had named them Eleanor because he had said how wonderful his daughter was. "Oh, my pretty companionable little Daughter, you will come to Father," he wrote her, "and what jolly games we will have together to be sure."

"When? When?" she wrote excitedly. It was almost more than she could bear to be apart from him. The answer was always "Soon."

Shortly before her tenth birthday, Eleanor's dream exploded. On the first day of August in 1894, her father went for a ride. There was an accident and he was thrown from his carriage. The shock aggravated his already weakened heart. Two weeks later he was dead and Eleanor Roosevelt was now an orphan.

Chapter 3

LIFE WITH GRANDMOTHER

GRANDMOTHER HALL had two homes. One was her winter residence in the city, an old brownstone house with horsehair-stuffed black sofas. The other was her country place for the summer near Tivoli. On the same day each spring and fall, regardless of the weather, she moved from one place to the other.

Grandmother Hall moved in this fashion because she disliked making decisions based on fact. Another thing she disliked was the task of raising her two orphaned grandchildren after she had raised five children of her own. Her own had grown up without discipline because her husband had insisted that she must be a hothouse flower and not take part in household matters. As for himself, Grandfather Hall did not work a single day in his life and spent much of his time in his library. Here, year after year until his death in 1880, he read and discussed religious books with ministers and scholars.

If she could not control her own children, Grandmother Hall thought, this was no reason why Eleanor and Hall had to be brought up the same way. Utter strictness became her rule, even though her own underlying nature was not that way at all. Early she developed the habit of saying "No" even before Eleanor finished making a request. From her bedroom, which she seldom left, Grandmother Hall issued orders that Eleanor take two hot baths a week and a cold sponge shower every morning. However, the maid found it difficult to climb the stairs before breakfast and test the water, so cold Eleanor quietly added warm water.

Grandmother was also convinced that her thin granddaughter might die of cold. The result was that Eleanor had to wear long heavy flannels from early fall until late spring. On top of her flannels she had to wear a flannel petticoat and then a dress. As for clothes for the gawky girl, Mrs. Hall made her wear made-over hand-me-downs from her own daughters. The style of the day called for long skirts and gowns. Eleanor's poor-fitting old dresses failed to cover her knees, and she was forever slumping. Instead of buying her suitable clothes, Grandmother tried to correct her round-shouldered walk by making her wear a steel brace. Wherever she went the shy, self-conscious girl felt all eyes were upon her, for besides her strange clothes and heavy brace she had to wear long, thick black stockings and high-laced shoes.

Mrs. Hall was especially concerned about Eleanor after her father's death, for the girl seemed to be living in a dream world. She refused to believe that her father was gone, and spent her days thinking about him. From the moment she crawled from bed in the morning and all through the day, she made up adventures with her hero. "I lived with him more closely, probably, than I had when he was alive," she said.

In order to bring Eleanor out of her unreal world, Grandmother Hall hired a French governess to take her on daily walks. However, Eleanor walked so fast that she left her far behind. Then alone she would continue her dream existence. Later, on her return, she would find her governess sitting in the shade of an elm tree and together they would walk the last few hundred feet back to the house. It was not until almost a year passed that Eleanor worked her own way out of the unreal world she had created.

The following fall Eleanor was sent to Mlle. Le Clerq, a New York schoolmistress who ran a school in her home. Here Eleanor learned to recite the New Testament in French. This was about all she learned, for Mlle. Le Clerq had little understanding of grammar or arithmetic. This was of little concern to Mrs. Hall, for she did not believe that girls should be educated. Girls should learn to sew and cook and dance and smile, she believed. Eleanor was also sent to a dancing school run by a Mr. and Mrs. Dodsworth. Here she learned the waltz and polka. In addition, Grandmother sent her to a ballet school, where she learned to dance on her toes and appeared as a willow tree in the school show.

In the spring all this stopped temporarily when Mrs. Hall moved to Oak Terrace, her large estate with the 14-bedroom house outside of Tivoli. Here she concentrated on teaching Eleanor to cook and sew. Madeleine, a maid, was assigned to teach the girl the fundamentals and Grandma built a little house in the woods near her own brick mansion where Madeleine could instruct Eleanor. When Madeleine scowled at the way she darned a sock, Eleanor knew she would next cut an enormous hole in the sock and ask her to do it again. "Many a tear I shed over this darning," said Eleanor.

Madeleine also taught her to cook a few simple dishes and how to scour pots and pans. When the job did not meet her strict standards, she pulled Eleanor's hair to show her disapproval. She was also responsible for Eleanor's appearance and for seeing to it that she got out of bed at five A.M. each day. Often she grew angry because the girl enjoyed sliding down the moss-covered roof of the icehouse and getting her white clothes covered with green.

Grandmother Hall censored Eleanor's reading. Eleanor was not permitted to read the same book on Sunday that she had begun on another day. If she began a book on

Sunday, she was not allowed to finish it until the next Sunday. "Sunday was indeed a day set apart from other days," said Eleanor, "and some of the things decreed by my grandmother I personally very much resented. I could not play games on Sunday. I had to sit on the uncomfortable little seat in my grandmother's large victoria and drive five miles to and from church." The continual bumping on the road made her pale and sick. Once home from church, a Sunday duty was to teach Biblical verses to the coachman's daughter.

Despite her poor schooling, Eleanor showed early a great desire for reading and self-improvement. She hid books under her mattress, despite Grandmother Hall's rule against reading in bed. Eleanor learned that if she asked Grandma questions about a book she was reading, that book mysteriously disappeared. Her grandfather's library was crammed with complicated books on religion. "I never wanted to read these books," Eleanor said, "though I remember shedding tears over the illustrations in the Doré Bible." She was instead fond of books about people in trouble, because she could relate them to herself. One of her favorite books was titled *Misunderstood;* another, *Without Family.* She also wept long and loud over Hale's *Man Without a Country.* Sometimes when she was able to escape from Madeleine and her grandmother, she spent time "sitting up in an old cherry tree or lying flat on my stomach in the grass reading Dickens or Scott."

She also spent some time looking after her yellow-haired little brother Hall, who was six years younger than she. A favorite pastime was to take him deep into the woods. Here she assumed the character of Robinson Crusoe, while he was her Man Friday. Her troubles were drowned out as they went from one adventure to another.

Eleanor's general loneliness was increased by the fact that she had no playmates her own age. Her grandmother permitted Carola de Peyster, whom Eleanor liked, to visit with her only one day each summer. When Eleanor was twelve, family friends asked Grandmother's permission to take her on a trip out West as company for their daughter. Mrs. Hall let out a sharp and loud "No!" and the matter was closed.

Mrs. Hall held a poor opinion of Eleanor's Roosevelt relatives, even after Uncle Ted's bravery as leader of the

Rough Riders in the Spanish-American War of 1898. Her claim was that the Roosevelts were noisy and not the least bit serious about the important things in life. The result was that only after much coaxing by Uncle Ted would she permit Eleanor to visit with his family at Sagamore Hill. Yet a weekend with Uncle Ted provided Eleanor with enough joy to last her for weeks afterward. He was so alive and warm, and was her closest link to her father. On her return home, Grandmother Hall always looked upon her as if she had come back from a terrible place.

It was better, Grandma thought, that she avoid noise and fun. She could go, however, to the Orthopedic Hospital in New York to talk to the poor crippled children and bring them presents. But she was not to walk too close to the beds because she was apt to pick up their diseases. She could also go with Aunts Pussie and Maude to the Bowery Mission and sing hymns to the derelicts who came there in search of food and lodging. Uncle Vallie, who was acceptable in the highest society and was a champion tennis player, went each Christmas to dress Christmas trees in Hell's Kitchen, the worst slum area in New York. Eleanor could help him, too. But what Mrs. Hall didn't know was that her son might dress just a tree or two and then disappear. Later Eleanor had to search for him in the dirty saloons along Third Avenue.

If she had a good friend, it was Mrs. Overhalse who did Grandmother's laundry. Mrs. Overhalse lived on a farm with her children, who numbered almost a dozen. Yet in addition to managing all her own responsibilities, she scrubbed all day for Grandma. She taught Eleanor to wash and iron, took her to her farm to eat her delicious German food, and showed by example that one could be cheerful even though burdened.

The important early teen years passed in this way. The hurt over her father was still with her, but more and more she wanted to do something worth while. Just what this might be for someone so poorly educated and shy, she could not imagine. But she would try to improve herself and be of help to others. "I am always questioning and questioning," she wrote in her diary, "because I cannot understand and never succeed in doing what I mean to do, never, never. I can feel it in me sometimes that I can do much more than I am doing and I mean to try till I do *succeed*."

When Eleanor was fourteen, her father's younger sister, Aunt Corinne, invited her to come during the Christmas holidays to a party for teen-agers. Grandmother Hall was reluctant to let her go because Aunt Corinne was a Roosevelt. But in the end she finally agreed.

Eleanor would have preferred that Grandmother Hall not let her go. For she had grown rapidly to almost her mature height of five feet eleven inches and she felt wretched wearing the made-over clothes that did not cover her knees. How could she talk to the other boys and girls when all the while they would be staring at her silly clothes? Besides, the boys and girls invited to Aunt Corinne's knew each other well. She would be an outsider. No one would want her company. Her mother had been right in calling her "Granny."

On this fateful night fifty young couples were poised for the orchestra's gay strains. The floor was highly polished. Suddenly the polka began and the lead couple came gaily down the center. On the sidelines Eleanor stood, her face ready to burst into a flood of tears. She tugged at her dress and felt sorry for herself.

She watched the lead couple as they sped through the intricate steps. The girl was Cousin Alice, Uncle Ted's daughter. The particularly handsome boy dancing with her was Franklin Roosevelt, her distant cousin Franklin from Hyde Park. What a look of pure joy he had on his

face. Eleanor had seen him briefly last year at her Cousin
Susie Parish's place. But he wouldn't know her now. How
could he remember her? And if he did, it would be only a
memory to laugh at because of her clothes.

The dance ended and the couples applauded before they
left the floor. Now they would stand about for a while
and laugh and talk until the next dance. Eleanor felt
more unhappy than before. Standing alone she rubbed
her hands together nervously and stared blankly ahead.
Her eyes finally moved among the couples and they stopped
at Franklin and Alice. She watched them smiling and jok-
ing until he turned and his gaze met hers for a fleeting
moment.

The orchestra was back in place and ready to begin the
next number. Franklin was leaving Alice and walking
across the dance floor. Eleanor hugged the wall to hide herself as much as possible. Suddenly he was in front of her,
facing her. "Eleanor," he asked with a friendly, warm
grin, "may I have the next dance with you?"

"Oh, Franklin," she almost shouted, "I'd love to!"

"Then let's." He offered his arm.

Around the floor they whirled. All the while he acted as
though he were enjoying himself, but her frightened mind
found this hard to believe. After the orchestra stopped, he
talked to her for a time, laughed and joked, thanked her
and moved on. Her holiday was a success.

A great change came in Eleanor's life when she was
fifteen. Grandmother Hall decided that instead of keeping
her under close watch it would be better if she left. For
her own children, whom she could not control, were too
gay and set a bad example for Eleanor. Uncle Vallie had
begun to drink too much. Once he came down the stairs
with a rifle and shot out the living-room windows. Eleanor
liked him a great deal when he was sober because he taught
her how to ride and jump. Sometimes in the fall after

Grandma moved back to the city, he would take her for
an outing to Oak Terrace at Tivoli. Once when they were
caught in a blizzard, Uncle Vallie acted heroically in keeping Eleanor warm and getting her food. Uncle Eddie, the
younger son of Grandmother Hall, was a mystery to
Eleanor because he was always disappearing without notice. Once he went to Africa without telling his mother
and she worried until he walked into the house and announced he would be at the table for dinner.

Then there were the two younger sisters of Eleanor's
mother, who were still at home. Aunt Maude took Eleanor
along for rides in her two-wheeled gocart. One day they
met their first automobile. The horse reared up and tried
to leap a barbed-wire fence. Eleanor was tossed yards away,
her head stunned and her short dress ripped. Aunt Pussie
was temperamental and high-strung. One day she would
play endless games of "I Spy" with Eleanor around the
piazza, read her poetry by the hour and build a campfire.
The next day she would ignore Eleanor's existence and not
speak to her. Once Pussie took Eleanor and her governess
to Nantucket Island for a vacation. But once arrived,
Aunt Pussie grew bored and left the two stranded there
without money. Only a crying appeal to Grandmother Hall
at Oak Terrace produced money to pay their fares home.

Her four remaining children at home were becoming too
much of a problem to Grandmother Hall. By example,
they undid the job she was attempting in raising Eleanor
and her little brother. Besides, in the last few months
Pussie had been acting strangely. For days on end she
locked herself in her room, and no one knew whether she
was alive or dead.

One day Grandma called Eleanor into her room for a
private talk. "It is about your future," she told her granddaughter with a deep sigh. "I have decided that you must

have further education away from here. Your mother
wanted you to go to a boarding school in Europe. And I
have decided to send you, child."

Thus ended Grandmother Hall's close control over
Eleanor.

Chapter 4

SCHOOLING ABROAD

IT was in the fall of 1899 when Eleanor crossed the
Atlantic to England. Auntie Bye, her Uncle Theodore
Roosevelt's older sister, prevailed upon Grandmother Hall
to let her study with the same teacher Bye had. Auntie Bye
had attended a school run by Mlle. Souvestre near Paris
in the years between the American Civil War and the
Franco-Prussian War of 1870. Mlle. Souvestre had helped
her overcome her own shyness because of her deformed
back. When she found her old teacher still alive and running a school in England thirty years later, she insisted that
Eleanor spend some years with her, too.

The school was called Allenswood, and was at South
Fields, close to Wimbledon Common and connected to
London by subway. When Eleanor arrived in her short
dress and full of concern over her appearance and lack of
schooling, she found Mlle. Souvestre both motherly and
soothing. The headmistress was a short and heavy woman,
with snowy white hair and delicate features. *"Ma chère
petite,"* she called the fifteen-year-old girl and put her at
ease.

But Mlle. Souvestre was concerned about Eleanor's shyness and her belief that she was homely. She went to great
trouble to help the girl. One of the first things she did was
to order Eleanor to stop wearing the ridiculous hand-me-
down dresses from her aunts. One of Eleanor's great thrills
was having a dress made to order for her in a stylish shop.

31

Mlle. Souvestre also forbade her to continue her nervous nail biting. On this issue she made no headway until Eleanor reread one of her father's letters that she had brought with her to England. In it, he stressed the importance of cleanliness and good habits, and she swore off nail biting.

Mlle. Souvestre ran her school according to strict rules. One was that the girls could speak only French. Anyone who spoke an English word had to report herself to the headmistress at the end of the school day. There were other rules for social deportment, for cleaning and airing one's room, and for bathing.

Girls who broke too many rules were expelled, though once when Eleanor was indirectly involved, Mlle. Souvestre had trouble deciding. Eleanor's first roommate was a girl with a violent temper to whom she was much attached. When the girl threw an inkwell at a teacher, who insisted she be expelled, Eleanor ran to Mlle. Souvestre in tears. "Give her another chance," Eleanor cried.

The old headmistress was torn between Eleanor's plea and the actual facts of the case. Finally after many sleepless nights she decided that if she gave in to Eleanor the girl would be after her from then on to save other girls. The result was that Eleanor's roommate was sent home.

In testing Eleanor, Mlle. Souvestre was shocked at her poor education to that point. But she recognized that she had a quick, eager mind and wanted to learn. If this were so, then the girl should carry a heavy load of studies. In a single term she had Eleanor taking French, German and Italian, as well as English history and literature, piano, violin and *danse*. One teacher, Miss Strachey, made her keep detailed notebooks on English and French literature. Mlle. Souvestre also insisted she work to strengthen her thin body. Every morning after breakfast she had to take a long walk on the common, and after lunch she was rushed through two hours of exercise. A happy day in her life at Allenswood came when she was named to the first hockey team. "I felt I was starting a new life," said Eleanor. "For the first time all my fears left me."

Eleanor worked hard at her studies to make up for lost time. In a few months she caught up with the best students at Allenswood and remained at that level. On each report card Mlle. Souvestre sent to Grandmother Hall, she wrote,

"Excellente élève" (excellent pupil). One of the things that interested her headmistress was how easy it was to tell what was on the girl's mind from the essays she wrote. Mlle. Souvestre thought her pretty, but Eleanor did not believe she was. Furthermore, Eleanor thought that character was more important than looks. In an essay on loyalty she wrote: "It may seem strange but no matter how plain a woman may be if truth and loyalty are stamped upon her face, all will be attracted to her and she will do good to all who come near her." Mlle. Souvestre was also impressed with Eleanor because she considered ambition a virtue. In another essay, Eleanor wrote: "Some people consider ambition a sin, but it seems to me to be a great good for it leads one to do and to be things which without it one could never have been."

One result of Eleanor's fine work was that she became a member of the small group of girls Mlle. Souvestre invited to her study in the evenings. It was here that Eleanor discovered she had an excellent memory and could repeat without error poems she heard for the first time. Mlle. Souvestre was especially impressed with Eleanor when grownups were present because she was able to pick their minds and later use their knowledge as her own.

Mlle. Souvestre was very outspoken on politics and public issues and invited her small select group to join her in discussions. Eleanor had never before questioned matters that did not concern her directly. She had always accepted the big world outside her own small existence as something not related to herself. "You are not a full person," said the headmistress, "unless you take an interest in what is going on in the world. You must not live for your own self but must strive to be of service to others." This was a new thought to Eleanor and it made her feel older because it gave purpose to her life.

In her timid way, on short trips to London she looked

at things she saw with new eyes. She saw the bad slums and the sickly children who lived there and wondered why others did little to improve life there. Once when she passed out her spending money to beggars, she wrote in her notebook: "Poor woman—$1." U S 1066611

Mlle. Souvestre also took Eleanor to France and Italy one Eastertime to help her develop more independence. Eleanor had to do the packing and unpacking for both as well as to make the travel arrangements and buy tickets. In several cities, Mlle. Souvestre made her go sightseeing alone. "For days," said the sixteen-year-old girl, "I would be turned loose in Florence, Rome, Paris, finding my way about, seeing what interested me and then going home and talking it over with Mademoiselle." When Eleanor asked why she didn't come with her, Mlle. Souvestre would smile and say she had seen the sights many times before.

Nevertheless, there were some bad moments for Eleanor. For instance, one day when she roamed about Paris alone, she bumped into family friends. "Eleanor, where is your chaperone?" they gasped. When she admitted she had none, they were anxious to depart. She guessed correctly that they couldn't wait to write Grandmother Hall about her bad carryings-on.

In the summer of 1901, Eleanor was abruptly called home by Grandmother Hall. "You've had enough schooling," she told her.

"But it has just begun," Eleanor cried.

The old woman was not convinced. "But you must prepare for your debut into society next year when you will be eighteen."

"I don't care about that. I want to go to school." The thought of leaving Mlle. Souvestre forever was a harsh blow.

In the end, after letting Eleanor mope all summer, Mrs. Hall relented. "You can return to Allenswood for one

more year and no longer," Grandmother ruled. "Then
you must return for your 'coming out.' "

Her third and final year at Allenswood passed swiftly.
President William McKinley had been assassinated in
1901, and Uncle Ted, who was his Vice-President, now
occupied the White House. As the niece of the President
of the United States, Eleanor was now a minor celebrity.
Mlle. Souvestre was happy because she thought that
Eleanor's new position would give her more self-confidence. Once some of the girls had their fortunes read in
London. When the fortuneteller heard Eleanor's name,
she told her quickly that one day she would live in the
White House as a President's wife. She blushed furiously
while the girls clapped their hands.

With summertime coming, Eleanor felt sad. She knew
that her wonderful years with Mlle. Souvestre were draw-
ing to an end and she dreaded leaving her. They made
another trip to the Continent and Eleanor tried to squeeze
as many pleasant moments into those days as she could.
Mlle. Souvestre was also sad, because she had grown quite
attached to this quiet girl. Toward the end of the school
year Eleanor wrote a story that told clearly her unhappiness
at leaving this wonderful teacher. "I sat all alone on the
beach," she wrote, "waiting for the sunset and watching
the waves as they rolled in and broke at my feet. Suddenly
I looked up. The fiery red ball was getting lower and lower
and just before it touched the sea I saw a beautiful woman
rise out of the water to meet it and she held out her arms
to it as though begging it to come nearer. Then she shook
out her golden hair till the whole sky became golden and
as she drew nearer the red light grew softer and softer and
blended itself with her hair and as she sank lower and lower
it sank with her and just as they kissed the water, her mass
of golden hair fell over her and hid her from my sight
and all that was left of my beautiful vision was a faint,

faint ripple of gold on the water and soon even that disappeared."

Eleanor left Allenswood in the summer of 1902, following a tearful farewell from her wise old teacher. Even before she was back in the United States, Mlle. Souvestre had written her grandmother: "Eleanor has had the most admirable influence on the school and gained the affection of many, the respect of all. To me personally I feel I lose a dear friend in her."

Chapter 5

COUSIN FRANKLIN

IT was the following fall and Eleanor was sitting in a coach seat on the New York Central on her way up the Hudson to Tivoli. On her lap was a history book, but the bumping and jerking of the old train made reading difficult.

She thought of her dear teacher Mlle. Souvestre and all that had happened to her since her return home. She had tried in vain to convince Grandma to let her go to college. "All you need, child"—the old woman had shaken her head—"are a few of the social graces to see you through life." Instead, Grandmother Hall had insisted that she make her social debut.

Her name had been put on almost all Social Register lists for debutante parties. The first was an assembly ball to which she had been escorted by her cousins, Mr. and Mrs. Henry Parish. In the ballroom all the young people knew each other, whereas she was a stranger. Luckily one of Uncle Ted's Rough Riders, a handsome young Englishman named Robert Ferguson, saw her plight and rounded up several other young men to dance with her. Another evening there was a large theater party in her honor and a dance at Sherry's in New York. She enjoyed wearing her fancy Parisian clothes, but such social life bored her.

It had not been all party-going. Grandmother Hall was now greatly concerned about her two sons, Vallie and Eddie, who were heavy drinkers. Eleanor could not have visitors because there was no telling when her uncles would enter the room and cause a scene. Once when she was especially lonely, she invited two girls to stay at Oak Terrace for a few days. "Every moment that they were there," she admitted, "I held my breath for fear some unfortunate incident would occur."

Eleanor's twelve-year-old brother Hall was afraid of Uncle Vallie. Finally, Grandmother Hall decided that Eleanor should enroll him at Groton in order to get him out of the house. Eleanor was to be responsible for Hall from then on and meet with his teachers and discuss his problems as if she were his mother. As for Eleanor, she would live with Aunt Pussie in the brownstone house in the city for a while and then move in with her cousins, the Parishes.

All these events Eleanor was thinking about when a handsome, yellow-haired young man came down the coach aisle and stopped alongside her seat. "Hello, Eleanor," he said. It was her fifth cousin, Franklin Roosevelt of Hyde Park.

"Hello, Franklin," she replied with a warm smile.

"So you remember me," he laughed, jutting his chin out.

"Certainly," she said, even though she hadn't seen him since the dance when she was fourteen. He was tall and thin and looked like the Harvard man that he soon told her he was. "How are your parents?" she asked, as he slid into the vacant seat next to her.

His face turned momentarily sad. "Father has been dead almost two years. But Mother is in the Pullman car," he added brightly. "Won't you come and meet her?"

Mrs. James Roosevelt was pleased to see Eleanor. She held her head high and her back straight as she talked about Eleanor's parents. "You must come and visit us," she told Eleanor when the train stopped at Hyde Park.

Eleanor next saw Franklin at one of the debutante dances. After that he began popping up at other "coming-out" parties. Then he asked her to a house party at Hyde Park. There were several pretty girls present, but he stayed with her most of the time. He was a junior at Harvard and he asked her to some of the football games.

That same fall Eleanor decided to do more than merely seek enjoyment at debutante parties. Though her grandmother opposed it, she joined the Consumer League, an organization of well-to-do women who were concerned about the wretched working conditions for women and children in the factories of New York. Timidly yet purposefully she went along with others to investigate sanitation and safety in several plants. She also joined the newly organized Junior League and taught dancing at the Rivington Street Settlement House. Rivington was in the midst of a filthy, crowded slum section of New York.

Once Franklin came to the Rivington Street Settlement House to pick her up after her dancing class. Her little pupils shouted out, "Is he your feller?" She blushed furiously while Franklin laughed.

Another time when one of the little girls took ill, she asked Franklin to help carry her home. When he saw the hovel where the child lived he gasped, "My gosh, I didn't know anyone lived like this!"

Franklin's childhood had been happy and he had led a sheltered life of ease. His father had been the director of several railroads and had married Sara Delano, the daughter of millionaire Warren Delano, who was engaged in the shipping trade with China. He had never known want, nor had Franklin ever seen poverty face-to-face.

In the fall of 1903 when Eleanor visited her brother at Groton School, Franklin met her there and proposed to her. She accepted him, but when he broke the news to his mother she was stunned. She insisted that he and Eleanor were too young to marry at twenty-one and nineteen.

When Eleanor learned of Sara Delano Roosevelt's opposition to her marriage, she wrote her a letter. "I know just how you feel and how hard it must be," she said. "But I do so want you to learn to love me a little. You must know that I will always try to do what you wish for I have grown to love you very dearly during the past summer."

Nevertheless, Sara Roosevelt insisted and they agreed to postpone any announcement for the time being. Franklin had so much to do as editor of the *Harvard Crimson,* she said, while Eleanor was enjoying herself in her social work activities. Why not continue as they were for a while and learn more about life?

In February of 1904, Sara Roosevelt took Franklin and his college roommate on a six-week cruise to the West Indies. She hoped that he would forget Eleanor during that time.

Meanwhile, Eleanor went to Washington to visit with Uncle Ted in the White House and with Auntie Bye, Uncle Ted's sister who lived nearby. At Auntie Bye's Uncle Ted would drop in during the evening and sit in the parlor with Eleanor and Bye and discuss the problems he faced as President. Eleanor was much in awe and said little. It was enough to be in his company and feel the warmth of his friendship. But Auntie Bye offered much advice to her brother. In turn, Uncle Ted considered his crippled sister among his closest advisers. He talked over with her the crisis between Japan and Russia, which was to lead to war in 1904; whether he should run for another term; and his fight against permitting single companies to win monopolies in their industries.

Meanwhile, Sara Roosevelt's six-week cruise with her son had come to an end. He had moped throughout the trip and she knew he had not forgotten Eleanor. Without knowing where Eleanor was, she brought Franklin to Washington with the hope of finding an overseas job for him. An old family friend, Joseph Choate, then American ambassador to Great Britain, was in Washington to consult with the State Department. She hurried to see him and begged him to take Franklin on as his secretary in the London Embassy. But he already had a secretary, he told her.

When Franklin discovered that Eleanor was in Washington, he rushed to Auntie Bye's by carriage as swiftly as he could. Sara Delano Roosevelt knew then that she could not keep the young lovers apart. "You have my blessing," she told Eleanor.

Uncle Ted was also pleased that Eleanor was to marry Franklin. He invited them to dinner at the White House. "Dee-lighted!" and "Bully," he crushed Franklin's hand with his powerful grip. "May I give the bride away at the wedding?" he asked Eleanor. When she nodded, he beamed.

During the meal, Uncle Ted rose and began pacing the dining room as he discussed a vexing problem of government. Franklin sat openmouthed and stared at him. "What a thrill it was to watch history in the making," he told Eleanor afterward.

They were married on St. Patrick's Day, March 17, 1905. Uncle Ted had insisted that they come to his Inauguration on March 4th, even though Eleanor was in the midst of her wedding preparations. They had sat on the Capitol stairs during the swearing-in ceremony, and Eleanor had watched Uncle Ted so intently while he made his inaugural address that she didn't hear a single word of his speech. Afterward, she and Franklin ate lunch with him at the White House and sat in the special box to watch the inaugural parade, which included a thousand marching Rough Riders and Geronimo, the captured Apache Indian.

All of New York's social leaders came to Eleanor's wedding. Many had trouble reaching the house of her cousin, Mrs. Henry Parish, where the wedding was held because of the mammoth St. Patrick's Day parade around the corner on Fifth Avenue. Also a huge crowd had collected on the corner to catch a glimpse of Theodore Roosevelt. Almost a hundred policemen in gray helmets and frock coats formed a human chain to keep the crowd back. Finally Uncle Ted came into the block in an open carriage and the crowd cheered wildly.

Eleanor was calm, but Franklin was so nervous before the ceremony that the Reverend Endicott Peabody, headmaster of Groton, who was to perform the wedding, had to take him into an alcove to calm him. As the "Wedding March" began, she came down the stairs with Uncle Ted. She wore the same white satin dress Grandmother Hall had worn at her own wedding plus jewelry her mother wore when she married Eleanor's father. The Irish shamrock in Uncle Ted's lapel was badly wilted, but a beaming smile sat on his face as he held her arm.

If the large crowd and the brassy band hadn't broken into the block past the police, the guests at the wedding might have heard the ceremony. But with the repeated choruses of "The Wearin' o' the Green," this was not possible. When the ceremony was over, Uncle Ted kissed the bride and congratulated Franklin. "I'm glad you are keeping the name in the family," he bellowed. Then he turned and Eleanor watched him stride into the library where tables were piled high with food.

Anxious to be near the President, the guests deserted Eleanor and Franklin and hurried into the library after him. When they were all alone in the room, Franklin looked at Eleanor, embarrassed, and said, "Well, we might as well join the party."

"Yes, let's," Eleanor laughed.

Uncle Ted had to leave early, for he had a speech to make. Eleanor watched from a window as the crowd outdoors yelled, "Three cheers for Teddy! Ain't he the real thing?" In fun, Uncle Ted shook a fist playfully at the ragged newsboys who rushed forward to touch their hero.

They could not go on their honeymoon until the following summer. Franklin had graduated from Harvard but he was now attending law classes at Columbia University in New York, and he had to wait until the term ended. Eleanor had hoped to show off her handsome husband to Mlle. Souvestre. Unfortunately, her beloved teacher died a few months before.

On her honeymoon, twenty-year-old Eleanor learned a few things about her husband as well as herself. For one thing, he suffered from nightmares and was a sleepwalker. Once, awakened by wild screams, she found they came from Franklin. "Don't you see the revolving beam?" he yelled. "Everyone must be awakened before they are all dead!" Another time, she found he had "turned over a chair and started to open the shutters!" She pulled him away from the open window as he started to climb out. "I must get it, it is very rare, the only one and a most precious book," he argued. The next morning he could not remember the episode.

In Scotland, he bought Eleanor a tweed coat which she still wore almost fifty-five years later. It was also in Scotland where Eleanor had her most embarrassing moment. "Tell me, my dear," a woman asked her, while others listened, "what exactly is the difference between your national and state governments?"

"Well, you see . . ." Eleanor began, only to fall silent. She had nothing to say. The niece of the President of the United States knew almost nothing about the American Government. Franklin came to her rescue and answered for her, but on the spot Eleanor told herself that when she returned home she would learn more about her Government. "Not only were women not supposed to know anything about their own government in those days," she said, "but they even prided themselves on their ignorance."

Mlle. Souvestre had opened her eyes to literature and history and the importance of being of service to others. But her growth could not stop there. It was up to Eleanor to develop her personality and interests further.

Chapter 6

WIFE AND MOTHER

ELEANOR was unprepared for marriage. She knew nothing about running a household or caring for children. After her first baby, Anna, was born, she put her out one day for a morning nap in a box outside the back window. When little Anna screamed and screamed, Eleanor remembered from something she had read, "A modern mother does not pick up a baby when it cries."

Two hours later when Anna was still screaming, the wall phone rang. "How dare you let a child cry like that?" an indignant voice bellowed. "I am going to report you to the Society for the Prevention of Cruelty to Children."

Eleanor took her infant indoors, realizing her own great shortcomings.

For her six children, she hired nursemaids. Most of them soon found out how little she knew about child care and ordered her about as well as the children. Several were Simon Legrees and punished her children, often unjustly. They would frown upon Eleanor with blazing eyes the few times she had the courage to object to their strong discipline. If only she had been too poor to hire nurses, she realized years later, "my children would have had far happier childhoods."

Instead, she and Franklin had inherited wealth and lived as others did in their class. From her father's estate she received $7,500 a year, while Franklin got $5,000 from his.

In addition, during those early years of marriage, her

mother-in-law continued to treat Eleanor as a child. She determined where Eleanor and Franklin would live, hired the servants, and insisted that Eleanor have at least one meal a day with her. After Eleanor had been married only a short time, Sara Roosevelt built twin houses in New York City, one for herself and the other for Franklin and Eleanor. Wall panels could be pushed aside on pulleys until both houses were one. The result was that Eleanor had no privacy. She also lost what little self-confidence she had, and it took years to regain it.

She made a sorry picture running to Franklin's mother for advice on almost every matter. "I never thought of asking for anything," she said, "which I felt would not meet with her approval." In 1907, Eleanor had her second child, James, and in 1909, another son whom she named Franklin, Jr. However, Franklin, Jr., caught the flu six months later and died. Eleanor was reminded all over again of her childhood sadness with the loss of her mother and father and little Ellie.

One evening Franklin came home from the law firm where he worked and found her sobbing. "What's the matter?" he asked, bewildered.

"I don't want to live in this house," she told him.

"But why not?"

"Because it isn't mine in any way. I had nothing to do with getting it and it isn't the kind of house I would have got."

"Now, now," Franklin tried to console her, realizing for the first time that Eleanor felt chained. "I think you are taking Mama too seriously." He loved his mother, but he realized that Eleanor needed independence. But this would have to come from within her, through her own efforts.

Another problem Eleanor had was that she believed that a wife should have the same interests as her husband. Franklin loved to collect rare books, stamps and ship models. She tried to interest herself in these and when they bored her, she thought there was something wrong with her. When Franklin built a golf course on the island of Campobello, where they had a summer cottage, she thought it necessary that she take up the game. On the sly she practiced, and one day announced that she would play with him.

For three holes she missed ball after ball and dug up his carefully seeded sod. Franklin's smile disappeared by the fourth hole. He stared at her beet-red face and said flatly, "Eleanor, why don't you take up some other sport?"

Another time, because he enjoyed driving cars, she learned how too. But coming into the yard one day, she demolished the gatepost and sheared off the corner of the porch. She was so upset by this accident that she did not drive again for years.

But the golf and auto experiences taught her an important lesson. It was not vital to have the same interests as Franklin. She must develop those that suited her best.

These years of early marriage saw also an important development in their lives. Before Uncle Ted left office in March 1909, she and Franklin visited him on occasion in the White House. Uncle Ted would brush his mustache and then turn fondly toward Eleanor to ply her with personal questions. "She is more like him than any of his own children," Aunt Corinne once observed. "Eleanor was always my Brother Ted's favorite niece."

She felt relaxed and comfortable in his presence, and as the evening wore on, he would turn eventually toward Franklin. "My boy," he would say in his toothy way, "why don't you get into politics? There is no higher calling than the public service where you work for the betterment of the lives of your fellow men."

Knowing that Franklin had voted for him in 1904, he urged him to become more active among the Republicans.

"I voted for him because he was a better democrat than the Democratic candidate," Franklin told Eleanor later. "I prefer the Democratic Party."

In 1910, Franklin decided to run for the New York State Senate as a Democrat for the district covering Hyde Park. His mother, who was a Republican, expressed immediate disgust at his going into politics at all—and as a Democrat!

Eleanor had never seen him happier, for he had not enjoyed being a lawyer. What did it matter that the district had sent only a single Democrat to the state senate since 1856? If he would try hard enough, she believed, he would win.

But he came home sad one day. Uncle Ted had taken over the New York Republican organization now that he was out of the White House. He had announced that he would tour the state in behalf of the Republicans. "If he speaks in this district," Franklin said, "I'm licked."

Eleanor sat down and wrote a letter to Auntie Bye about Franklin's concern. Back came a letter from Uncle Ted. "Franklin ought to go into politics without the least regard as to where I speak or don't speak. He's a fine fellow."

She had another son, Elliott, in September, so she did not take part in the campaign. However, she went to hear him speak one time. It was the first time she had seen him on a political platform and she thought he looked thin and nervous. The blood seemed to have been drained from his face and he was expressionless. His slow-speaking manner made her wince. As for his wooden gestures, Mlle. Souvestre would have given him a long scolding. "I know I am no orator, but . . ." he apologized at one point.

"You don't have to be an orator, Roosevelt!" someone in the crowd shouted back and the crowd cheered. Eleanor felt better.

Once when he tried to jump on a moving streetcar to

rush to his next speaking engagement, he fell off. He was
bloody and his clothes were torn. But Eleanor stayed up
twenty-four hours like a Florence Nightingale to soak his
torn arm and leg with disinfectant, and he limped back
to the campaign.

In the end, it was worth all the agony. For he won and
Eleanor sensed they were starting a new phase in their
lives.

Whereas Eleanor was sensitive and quiet, Franklin was
outgoing and loved a battle. When they moved to Albany
for the session of 1911, she was twenty-six and he almost
twenty-nine. Reporters called him the "baby" of the legislature. They hardly expected to hear from him once the
session began. But they were wrong.

At that time there was no direct election of United
States senators. State legislatures decided who would go to
the Senate in Washington. In New York in 1911, the state
legislature had to name a new U.S. Senator for the six-year
term beginning March 4th. New York Democratic political
bosses organized in the body called Tammany Hall controlled the majority in the state legislature. They decided
that the next U.S. Senator would be their man, William
"Blue-Eyed Billy" Sheehan from Buffalo.

"No," Franklin told Eleanor. " 'Blue-Eyed Billy' is just
a Tammany hack and has no business going to the Senate."

Quietly he organized a group of eighteen state senators
who felt as he did. With the support of the Republicans
in the state senate they could defeat Sheehan, he insisted.
"The rights and wrongs of that fight meant very little to
me," said Eleanor.

Nevertheless, she opened her house as the small group's
headquarters. Here they came to plot and give each other
courage. They came in the morning to map that day's
strategy; then went to vote No on Sheehan; then returned
to her house to talk long past midnight. For three months

this went on. Franklin explained to a reporter, "We just sit around and swap stories like soldiers at the bivouac fire." In time the house got so stuffy with cigar smoke that Eleanor moved Anna, James and Elliott to third-floor bedrooms because it sickened them. Eleanor sat in the midst of the group, the only woman present, and now and then she expressed a quiet opinion. Years later, Franklin claimed that her "political sagacity" had its beginning at these anti-Sheehan sessions.

The fight ended in victory for Franklin when Sheehan withdrew as a candidate. But Eleanor was shocked at what happened to some in Franklin's group. "One man owned a small country newspaper, largely dependent for existence on government printing and the advertising of local merchants. He also had a wife and two children." He was told by Tammany that they would ruin his paper. He lost his government printing contracts and "local merchants found it 'wise' to withdraw their advertising. He was a ruined man."

At this point, there was little about politics that Eleanor liked.

However, the Sheehan fight made her husband a national figure, and it was obvious to her that politics was to be their life. In 1913, Franklin was appointed Assistant Secretary of the Navy by President Woodrow Wilson, and Eleanor moved to Washington with her family. Here she was to remain through the two terms of President Wilson. Franklin had great pride in holding this post because Uncle Ted had once held the same position. After he was sworn in, he wrote his mother about his new job. Back came the reply: "Try not to write your signature too small as it gets a cramped look and is not distinct."

In Washington, Eleanor was terrified that she might do something to disgrace her ambitious young husband. Auntie Bye, into whose Washington house Eleanor moved with

Franklin and the children, offered her shy niece some advice. Auntie Bye looked into her troubled face and said, "No matter what you do, some people will criticize you. But if you would not be ashamed to explain your action to someone you loved, then you need never worry about criticism, nor need you ever explain what you do." This advice Eleanor followed throughout her life.

As Assistant Secretary, Franklin at thirty-one had to oversee the work in Navy yards throughout the country, purchase supplies and build training camps for sailors. Sometimes Eleanor accompanied him on inspection trips. Once on a trip to Navy yards and ports along the Gulf of Mexico, they were so busy that they could get only a few hours of sleep each night. Others in the party gave up under this grueling pace, but she and Franklin surprisingly did not collapse. Their endurance was extraordinary and was to come in handy in future years.

There was one problem, however, she could not solve at that time. She fell easy prey to seasickness. Once she accompanied Franklin to naval target practice in Chesapeake Bay. With a rough, chopping sea, it was only minutes before her face began turning green. A young officer strolling by on deck mistook her expression for boredom. "How would you like to climb the skeleton mast?" he asked enthusiastically. He pointed to a hundred-foot mast with a ladder climb to its top. "You will be able to see things much better from up there," he said.

"I suppose I could," she replied. What difference did it make that it was a vertical 100-foot climb? It was better to die like that than disgrace her husband. Miraculously, when she reached the top, her seasickness disappeared. "But it took me many more years," she said, "before I ceased to dread dinner or luncheon on board a battleship."

There was an important new member of their political family who was to stay with them until his death. This was a wizened little newsman named Louis Howe, whom Franklin had appointed as his assistant in the Navy Department. Howe had covered Albany for a New York paper and had known the Roosevelts since the time of the "Blue-Eyed Billy" Sheehan fight. Howe looked sickly with his bulging eyes, pockmarked face and chronic cough. He was never without a cigarette between his blistered lips and his most common ashtray was his greasy vest. His nails were chewed ragged and his collar flopped sweaty and wilted. But Franklin called him a political genius and would not do without him. Eleanor's reaction was that he was a "dirty little man" who dirtied a room within a minute after entering. When Howe told her that "Franklin will be President of the United States some day," she frowned in reply. Little did she realize then what an important role Louis Howe would play in her own life as well as in Franklin's.

A catastrophe was taking shape in Europe. In 1914, war broke out and soon England, France and Russia were fighting against Germany and the Austro-Hungarian Empire. Franklin was given the job of building up the American Navy. It was the hope of President Wilson to show other nations that the United States was strong, so that they would not attack this country. Franklin discussed all his problems with Eleanor and asked for advice, even though he knew that she hated war.

War came on April 2, 1917, after ruthless German submarine attacks on American shipping. Uncle Ted showed up at Eleanor's house one day. He wanted Franklin to use his influence to help him convince President Wilson to let him raise a division of volunteers and lead them overseas. Wilson would not agree and, said Eleanor, "Uncle Ted returned in a very unhappy mood. I hated to have him disappointed and yet I was loyal to President Wilson."

Eleanor's last two children, Franklin, Jr., and John, had

been born in 1914 and 1916, and she felt free now to help her country during the war. She knitted dozens of woollies and sweaters for Navy boys. She also made regular visits to naval hospitals to take on any needed task. Often she talked to the sick and wounded young men and brought them gifts. One woman wrote her about her son: "He never forgot the ice-cold lemon jelly and little cakes you brought him when you found he had no appetite." She also slaved sixteen hours a day, two or three days a week, in an iron cook-shack Red Cross canteen in the Washington railroad yards. Here she mopped floors in temperatures near 100 degrees, made sandwiches and coffee and passed them out to soldiers coming through Washington. Toward the end of the war, Franklin returned from a front-line inspection with an almost fatal case of the flu. When her children and the servants also caught it, Eleanor nursed them, too. Franklin was horrified to learn that in the evening, when everyone had been dosed, she would slip out to nurse government girls who were sick and alone in Washington.

After the war ended, Eleanor accompanied Franklin to Europe where his job was to close all American naval installations. On the way across, word came on January 6, 1919, of Uncle Ted's death. The announcement was a great shock to her, for outside of Franklin there was no man to whom she had been closer in the past twenty years. She could not find the right words for her diary as she wept. "Another great figure off the stage," she finally wrote.

They returned from Europe on the *George Washington* with President and Mrs. Wilson. One day at sea, Eleanor lunched with the President. He expressed pleasure at Franklin's fine work in Europe, but he glowed in talking about his own handiwork, the League of Nations. All the nations on earth would combine to prevent future wars. "The United States must join," Wilson told her, "or it will break the heart of the world. For she is the only nation that all feel is not out for gain and all trust."

The United States was destined never to join the League of Nations. Needing the approval of two-thirds the vote of the United States Senate, Wilson was never able to muster this number.

In 1920, the Democrats nominated Franklin as their Vice-Presidential candidate in a last attempt to win national support for the League. Eleanor went along on his campaign swing while he defended the League and attacked the Republican ticket of Warren Harding and Calvin Coolidge.

She learned a great deal by watching Franklin and Louis Howe in action. Franklin made more than ten speeches a day while the "dirty little man" with the chronic cough worked like a beaver on those speeches to give them life. It was the duty of the candidates' wife to sit close to her husband when he addressed a gathering. She was supposed to stare at him as if every word he uttered were a jewel and a surprise to her, even though she had heard the identical speech a dozen times before. She found it difficult to do this, especially since she worked with Howe on some of Franklin's speeches.

From the faces in their audiences, Eleanor judged that the people of the United States were not convinced of the benefits of the League of Nations. She was proved right when the Democrats were swamped in the November election.

For the first time since 1910 Franklin was out of politics and she was glad. It had been a hard ten years, and now that they had put in so much time in the public service it would be good to sit back and relax.

Chapter 7

THE SWAN EMERGES

THEY were now pursuing a normal life away from
the public spotlight. Franklin had begun to practice law
again and he was also the vice-president of the Fidelity
and Deposit Company of Maryland. Eleanor's existence
was now divided between her New York home and the
expanded Hyde Park home of her mother-in-law. In the
summer, she took her family to Campobello, the small
island between New Brunswick, Canada and Maine.

They were at Campobello on August 10, 1921. Eleanor
and the children went sailing with Franklin aboard their
boat, the *Vireo*. On their way back to shore, her oldest son,
Jimmy, spotted a forest fire on an island off Campobello.
"Of course," said Eleanor, "we must make for shore at
once and fight the fire."

It took several hours before the fire was out. By that
time they were all sweaty and grimy. The smell of smoke
was in their hair. "How about a race across the island and
a swim in Lake Glen Severn?" Franklin called out eagerly.

They took him up and started off across the island.
After the swim, eleven-year-old Elliott demanded that they
all dive once into the freezing Bay of Fundy. Franklin
didn't want to, but when the children clamored he agreed.
When they returned to their summer place, he told Eleanor
that he felt tired.

"Go lie down," she told him. But he ignored her and
sat in his wet bathing suit while he read a batch of mail
that had come in that day.

After a while when Eleanor glanced at him, she saw that his lips were purple and he was shivering. "You must go to bed immediately and get warm," she told him. "And don't do anything tomorrow."

"But I've promised the children that we're going camping tomorrow."

"You should be better by then," she said.

However, the next day he felt much worse. He had a fever and complained of aching joints. The local doctor who came at her call diagnosed his trouble as a bad cold.

The next day Franklin felt worse. When he rose from bed, his legs failed to support him and he fell. He let out a yell and Eleanor came running. Anxiously, she helped him back into bed. His trouble was no longer minor.

Three days later she wrote worriedly to Franklin's half brother Rosy: "We have had a very anxious few days as on Wed. evening Franklin was taken ill. It seemed a chill but Thursday he had so much pain in his back and legs that I sent for the doctor. By Friday evening he lost the ability to walk or move his legs but though they felt numb he can still feel in them. Yesterday I decided we wanted the best opinion we could get quickly so Louis Howe (who, thank heavens, is here, for he has been the greatest help) went with Dr. Bennett to Lubec and they canvassed the nearby resorts and decided the best available diagnostician was the famous old Dr. W. W. Keen of Philadelphia."

Dr. Keen's diagnosis proved to be wrong. He said that Franklin suffered from a small clot of dried blood that had settled temporarily in the lower spinal cord. It was important, he said, to massage Franklin's legs, and Eleanor and Louis Howe put in hours on end rubbing and pressing.

Actually, this was the worst thing they could have done, for Franklin had polio. When he continued in great pain, Eleanor called Dr. Robert W. Lovett, the Boston expert on infantile paralysis. Dr. Lovett's quick diagnosis was the polio that Eleanor had feared.

It was pathetic to look at Franklin in bed with a useless lower torso. Only a few years before, Walter Camp, the great Yale coach, told reporters, "Mr. Roosevelt is a beautifully built man, with the long muscles of the athlete." What future was there for him now? Eleanor worried.

Louis Howe made certain that news of Franklin's polio did not reach the papers. "If it does right now," he told Eleanor, "it will have a terrible effect on his political future."

"Do you really believe that Franklin has a future in politics?" she asked in amazement. She had been sleeping on a couch in Franklin's room and acting as nurse on 24-hour duty. Why would any man wracked with such pain and with two paralyzed legs want to go back into politics?

"Let me tell you what I believe." The little man let ashes drip from his cigarette to his vest. "I still believe that your husband will one day be President of the United States."

When Sara Roosevelt heard about Franklin's illness, she rushed immediately to Campobello. "My son must come home to live in Hyde Park," she told Eleanor. "He is going to be an invalid the rest of his life and he needs rest and complete quiet."

Franklin lay in bed and listened.

"That's the last thing he should do," Eleanor said. "And I won't let him."

Franklin's mother turned to Louis Howe for support. "You have good common sense, Louis. Can't you see that a political future is now out of the question for my son? He always wanted to write and when he comes home to Hyde Park, he can keep busy doing that or reading books or collecting stamps."

Louis Howe frowned. "I expect him to be President." Then turning toward Franklin, he said, "Sure you can retire and become a country squire like your father, or you can take up where you left off and go right on. So far as I'm concerned you're a man of destiny."

Eleanor watched her husband smile.

"I ought to know what is best for my son," the older woman cut in. "Those wild political friends will sap his strength."

Eleanor turned wearily to Dr. George Draper, a college classmate of Franklin's who was now his doctor. "What about it, George? Should Franklin spend his life in a wheel chair?"

Dr. Draper stared at her and at Franklin's mother. Whatever he said would be final. Eleanor pleaded with her blue eyes. Finally Dr. Draper said, "His recovery will be speeded if he becomes active again. He isn't an invalid and there is no reason why he should be treated as one."

Thank you, Eleanor told him silently.

Louis Howe wanted to sneak Franklin back to New York. "If the papers say he has infantile paralysis before we can break the news gently, Franklin is finished. Why, people think infantile paralysis is a disease affecting the mind."

Louis told reporters that Franklin would come to Eastport, Maine, by boat at a certain time and dock at a specific pier. However, he had the boat come in at another dock on the opposite side of Eastport. Eleanor sat with her five children in the bow of the motorboat while Franklin was cushioned on the floor boards. Though in deep pain, he managed to smile at them between groans. When the boat docked, he was lifted onto a baggage cart and carried to a private railroad car in a siding. Eleanor walked alongside him and whispered words of encouragement. Then his stretcher was passed into the car through a window. Finally when he was in bed and Eleanor had wiped his perspiring face, Howe told the reporters where he was and they came to see him.

In New York, when Franklin was ready to leave the hospital for his home, Howe finally broke the news to reporters. "No one need have any fear of permanent injury from this attack."

The next few months were the worst, though Eleanor knew that her husband was not a man to give up. It pained him to have anyone touch his bed sheets. Yet when plaster casts were on both legs and wedges were driven in deeper each day to stretch the leg tendons, he took pride in his ability to turn over.

But Sara Roosevelt would not give up. She was determined that Franklin must come home to Hyde Park and be her own invalid boy. She told Franklin constantly that he would always be a helpless cripple. She also pitted the children against Eleanor and Louise Howe. Eleanor had given Louis the big bedroom on the third floor and the children were put into small rooms on the fourth floor. "It isn't fair to you," Grandmother told fifteen-year-old Anna, "that you should have such a small room while that man has such a big room on the third floor. Besides, he has a bathroom, while you don't."

Once when Franklin was able to sit in a wheel chair, he supervised Anna as she put books into the library wall. When she dropped several, he scolded her and she ran off sobbing to her mother.

Eleanor Roosevelt put her arms around her daughter. "Mother talked of the battle Father was fighting against great odds," said Anna, "of the naturalness of his nervous reaction; how lucky we were to have him alive and to be able to help him get well; how much more patience and grit he had to have than we; until I felt very sheepish and even more ashamed—but in a different way, a more adult, understanding way. Back I went to the library where, of course, I not only found forgiveness, but also a sincere and smilingly given invitation to resume my place on the ladder."

Franklin tried everything to regain the use of his legs. It took him two years before he could move his big toe. "That was the hardest job I ever had to do," he told Eleanor. He tried walking on crutches, hanging on to parallel bars and riding a big tricycle. He taught himself to crawl on the floor like a baby. "The experience," said Eleanor, "gave him a strength and depth that he did not have as a young man. As he came gradually to realize that he was not going to get any better, he faced great bitterness."

"It's rather humiliating," Franklin told her, "to contract

a disease of which seventy-five per cent of the victims are
children."

It was time now to bring Franklin back into the world
that existed outside his sickroom, Louis Howe told Eleanor.

"How are you going to do that?" she asked.

Howe laughed. "I know the best way to get him back
into what he must be doing. You're going into politics.
He'll be jealous."

"Me?" She pointed at herself, as if it were a huge joke.

"That's right," Howe repeated. "You are going into
politics."

The mother of five and the wife of a cripple soon realized
that Louis Howe meant business. Though she was "upper
class," he made her join the Women's Trade Union
League, an organization interested in the welfare of women
workers. "You can learn a lot from some of those women,"
he told her.

Two of the leaders of the WTUL became good friends
of Eleanor's. "Bring them home to Franklin," Howe
growled, and she did. Franklin came alive and his eyes
sparkled as he argued with them. To Eleanor they were
a tonic, too.

At Howe's insistence, she also joined the Women's Division of the Democratic State Committee. She was asked
to speak at a fund-raising luncheon, but the thought of
rising and addressing a large group of people frightened
her. "Do it," ordered Louis Howe. "You need speaking
experience and it is better to learn with a little subject
and not a big one."

Somehow she got through it, though she felt clammy
and nervous. She must have been effective because she
raised $12,000. But Louis Howe did not think she had done
well. He had been sitting at the rear of the room listening
to her. "Why did you laugh when you were making a
serious talk?" he bellowed at her afterward.

She hadn't even known she had laughed.

"It's a nervous laugh," he told her. "And why did you go into a high-pitched giggle between sentences? Don't do it again."

She spoke often after that, driven by Howe. Sometimes he wrote her speeches and made her memorize them. After a while, he told her to strike out for herself. "Keep this in mind and you won't go wrong," he warned her. "Have something to say, say it, and then sit down!"

He also showed her how to read a newspaper. "Read the first paragraph of a story and it will give you a good summary. Don't waste time reading further unless it is of importance." He practiced going through entire papers with her page by page and scolded her until she could handle *The New York Times* in thirty minutes.

But she did not mind his scolding, for she was becoming interested in politics and wanted to improve herself. Besides, she was growing fond of the little gnome. While he was often cruel to her in teaching her about politics, in other matters he was always kind. "I remember," she said, "Louis Howe taking me out to dinner at a restaurant, sitting at a table he did not like, and eating food he did not like, simply because he knew I would be uncomfortable if he changed to another table or complained about the food."

Her progress was rapid. Only a year after her first speech, she was chairman of the finance committee of the Women's Division of the State Democratic Party. She also edited the Women's Division paper. Though she had no journalistic experience, Louis Howe taught her how to make up the sheets and proofread. "Louis wrote every headline," she admitted, "because he thought mine were terrible." But it wasn't many months before she was an old hand as an editor.

By now the sight of his wife as she moved about easily

among politicians made Franklin positively jealous! Politics was a man's game and was he not a man? he asked Howe. He would show Eleanor how good a politician he was. Sitting slouched on the chair next to Franklin's carved double bed, Louis let the ashes drop from his cigarette and smiled.

"At home we began discussing politics heatedly," said Eleanor about the change in him. He started holding receptions for the political leaders in New York and joined in talks on strategy.

Louis Howe wanted Eleanor to become friendly with Governor Al Smith, and she did. At one political convention she read a speech Louis had written in favor of Smith. "Al Smith is going places in politics," Howe told her, "and any personal link with him is important to Franklin."

Once Smith wrote Franklin, "I was awfully pleased to hear from Mrs. Roosevelt of the progress you are making. I just got all worked up over it."

In 1924, when Smith wanted to be the Democratic Party's candidate for President, he asked Franklin to make his nominating speech before the Democratic National Convention. Their campaign to bring Franklin back into politics was a great success, Louis Howe gleefully told Eleanor when he heard the news. Franklin accepted quickly, though he let his wife know about his doubts as to how he would reach the speaker's platform.

"It's his big test," Louis said to Eleanor later. "He cannot be carried up on the platform. If people see him being carried, they'll have only pity for him and he'll be dead politically."

If somehow Franklin got to the speaker's stand and made a forceful speech, Eleanor knew, he would be accepted once again as an active politician. It would do a great deal, too, for his mental health to feel independent and not helpless.

Unknown to the crowd and out of its view, Louis had Franklin pushed in a wheel chair to the speaker's platform. Finally his time came to go up and talk.

Eleanor watched, her hands clammy and her breathing uneven. With crutches under his arms and holding onto her seventeen-year-old son Jimmy, he swung himself along slowly toward the stand. A hush fell over the large audience as it waited to see if he could make it. And when he finally did, Eleanor took a deep breath and smiled with pride. For almost five minutes the crowd stood and cheered him.

And after he spoke for Smith and called him the "Happy Warrior," the delegates went completely wild. Louis Howe jumped up and down and screamed himself hoarse. Franklin was definitely on the road back.

Eleanor might have relaxed now and dropped out of her new activities. But she found them exciting. Her cousin, Theodore Roosevelt, Jr., whom she liked personally, was running that year for governor on the Republican ticket. She and Louis Howe handled the campaign against him and defeated him. On election day she drove people to the polls. She was shocked at how many sold their votes for money. One old man told her proudly that he had sold his vote several times during that day.

"But you are selling your right to be an equal with all other citizens," she said.

He smiled. "I vote as I please in the end anyway."

A new job she took on was to travel from town to town as a political organizer in behalf of women. Local Democratic leaders were not permitting women to serve on their local councils and she worked to change this. Once when she and another woman called on a local party leader, she was told by the man's wife that he was not at home. "That's all right," Eleanor told her, "we'll just wait on your porch until he returns."

An hour later the woman reappeared to watch Eleanor and her friend as they quietly sat knitting. "I don't know when my husband will be home," she said, annoyed.

"It doesn't matter," Eleanor laughed. "We haven't anything else to do. So we'll wait."

Another hour went by. Finally the door creaked open and a man's face appeared. "You win," he said glumly. He had been hiding indoors all the time. Eleanor smiled and proceeded to win his support for adding local women to his committee.

Louis Howe was pleased that his prodding was not a faucet that Eleanor could turn off. She showed remarkable talent as an administrator and several organizations begged for her assistance. She knew how to organize an activity and keep her fellow workers enthusiastic and working at their top ability. In 1926, she campaigned for Robert Wagner, who was running for the United States Senate. She traveled throughout the State of New York, organized women to work for Wagner's election and made several speeches for him. After Wagner won, he said he did so chiefly because of her efforts. She was also an excellent witness before committees of the state legislature on issues involving women, minority groups, the aged, and children.

Combined with all these activities was her full home life. Since her husband could not take part in outdoor activities with the children, she had to be both mother and father to them. First she joined the Y.W.C.A. Here she learned to overcome her fear of water that she had developed at Sagamore Hill where Uncle Ted threw non-swimmers off the dock. She also overcame her dislike of horseback riding so she could join her children, who were excellent horsemen. Driving a car was next on her list, though the first time she took the family out for a ride she backed off a steep hill and was saved only by a stout tree that stood in her path. Sometimes she took the children on long camping trips. On one, when Franklin Jr. cut himself with an ax, she calmly gave him first aid and he was soon none the worse for his injury.

At home the entire family, with the exception of his mother, talked to Franklin as though nothing ailed him. He roughhoused on the floor with his boys, worked busily with his hobbies, and through Eleanor and Louis Howe, kept in touch with political leaders in the state. "We didn't do anything," said Eleanor, "except treat him as a perfectly normal, able-bodied man which was what he made all of us feel he was."

Eleanor was happy with Franklin's ability to ignore his mother's pleas that he take to an invalid's bed. However, she was not pleased with Sara Roosevelt's continual interference with the raising of her children. The old woman loved her grandchildren to the point where she undid whatever disciplining Eleanor enforced. When the younger boys misbehaved, Eleanor gave their small pony away. Sara Roosevelt immediately bought them swift horses. When one of her boys wrecked an inexpensive car in a careless accident, his grandmother bought him a new, expensive model. Eleanor and Franklin gave the children small allowances in order to encourage them to earn extra money by doing farm chores. Sadly they found that Franklin's mother was giving them far more money than they.

Despite the old woman's activities, the Roosevelts remained a closely knit family. Everything was geared to helping Franklin improve. Late in 1924, Eleanor went with her husband to Warm Springs, Georgia. Here there was a swimming pool whose waters had a high concentration of mineral salts and was a natural 88 degrees. Franklin found that swimming in this water made his legs stronger. After a few years he was able to walk stiffly

with braces on his legs as he held on to someone alongside
for support. He was so impressed with his own limited im-
provement that he started the Warm Springs Foundation
to help others, especially children, who had polio.

By 1928, Eleanor was pleased with Franklin's progress,
though she knew he would never walk again. As for her,
she had become the best-known woman in the State of New
York. It was to be a big year for both.

Chapter 8

THE GOVERNOR'S WIFE

DESPITE Franklin's "Happy Warrior" speech for Al Smith at the Democratic National Convention in 1924, Smith had not won the Presidential nomination. That fall Smith had run for re-election as Governor of New York and had won. In 1928, however, Governor Smith won his party's nomination for the Presidency.

When he did he called Eleanor Roosevelt to his office. "I want you to head up all women's activities in the campaign for me," he told her. She agreed to do this.

Her job meant traveling outside her state to organize women Democrats, developing speaking and publicity programs. Her office staff knew her as a demon for work. She packed as many women visitors into Democratic headquarters in New York as space allowed. Here they were treated to tea, brief talks and handshakes with prominent women politicians. Once she insisted that Mrs. Nellie Ross, who had been Governor of Wyoming, appear for a long handshaking session. In the midst of it, Mrs. Ross disappeared. Eleanor found the Lady Governor lying on the floor of the ladies' rest room in a state of exhaustion.

In the fall of 1928, she took the time to go to Rochester for the State Democratic Convention. Al Smith was there searching for a strong candidate to succeed him as governor. He wanted her husband to run because he thought that Franklin's popularity would add to his own Presidential total in New York.

Franklin was then in Warm Springs. "Please call him for me and ask him to run," Smith asked Eleanor.

"I won't be used to make Franklin run," she told him. But when he insisted that she ask Franklin if he would consider, she put in a long-distance call to Georgia. "Yes, I know, Franklin," she told her husband. "I did tell the Governor you wouldn't run."

"I'm not well enough to run and that's all there is to it," said Franklin. "I need a few more years at least."

She put Al Smith on the phone, but he made no progress. After he hung up, he turned to Eleanor and asked, "Tell me for sure, do you think campaigning would ruin his health?"

"I don't know," she admitted. "The doctors feel that if he continues with his exercises and swimming at Warm Springs he might improve."

"Is it that he wants to walk before he will run?"

She smiled at his joke and that ended their talk.

By the next day word got out about Smith's desire to have Franklin run and the convention clamored for a final decision. Smith came back to see her. "Would you be willing to put in another call to your husband so we can try one more time?"

She told Smith she would do nothing further than say hello and turn over the phone to him. But it wasn't so easy to make connections. Franklin had expected a second call and had gone to Manchester, Georgia, where he did not believe he could be reached. Eleanor had a messenger climb the three flights to the school auditorium where he was making a speech and tell him to come to the town drugstore's phone. She would be waiting for him on the other end of the line.

It was more than an hour before he got there. "Hello, Franklin," she told him.

He laughed. "I've been keeping out of reach all day and I wouldn't have talked to anyone else but you—"

"I'm calling because Governor Smith begged me to. He's here beside me and I'm leaving you to him because I have to catch the train now for New York."

With that she handed the receiver to Smith. The last thing she heard as she rushed from the room was Smith yelling, "Hello, Frank!"

The morning paper brought her the news. Franklin had been persuaded to run for governor. She had hoped that he would not. She sent him a wire: REGRET THAT YOU HAD TO ACCEPT BUT KNOW THAT YOU FELT IT OBLIGATORY.

Louis Howe was furious when he heard. He slapped his forehead and let out an enraged roar. His timetable called for Franklin to run for governor in 1932, not 1928.

"You can't plan every move in this world," she told him. "You have to accept circumstances and make the best of them."

"You don't have to accept circumstances," he roared. "You dominate circumstances, that's what!"

There was only a four-week campaign in the governor's race. When Franklin came home to start his campaign, his mother greeted him with: "But you haven't the strength to run for office, my boy."

Louis Howe and Franklin went off on their own, while Eleanor concentrated on Smith's campaign against Herbert Hoover. She heard from him and Louis from time to time about the large crowds that greeted them everywhere. But she knew that many who turned out to greet a campaigner often did not bother to vote.

On election night Eleanor went with Franklin and his mother to his campaign headquarters in the Biltmore Hotel in New York City. Almost from the start Al Smith was running behind Herbert Hoover and Franklin behind his opponent, Albert Ottinger. By midnight, Smith was swamped by Hoover, while Ottinger had a substantial lead over Franklin. The early-morning papers hailed Ottinger as "Governor."

Eleanor left with Franklin, who was saddened by the returns. "Come along, Mama," she said to her mother-in-law.

But the old woman refused to go. "I'm going to stay right here until it is all over and you are Governor," she insisted to Franklin.

During the night late returns put Franklin in the lead. At sunrise, Sara Roosevelt rapped on Eleanor's door and awakened her. "I told you we have a governor in the family," she said proudly. It was true. While Smith had lost the state by more than 100,000 votes, Franklin had carried it by 25,000.

They spent four years in the creaking Executive Mansion in Albany. During that time Eleanor was the busiest woman in the state. Louis Howe had done his work well. He had taken the frightened and shy woman and had pushed her out into the busy world, watched her stammer and giggle nervously, and taught her so thoroughly that she changed into a strong, independent person.

Her weeks were fantastically crowded. With two other women she constructed a furniture factory called Val-Kill, about two miles from her mother-in-law's Hyde Park estate. Val-Kill was a non-profit venture to create jobs for unemployed skilled workers. Here they made reproductions of early American furniture. Eleanor also bought a part interest in the Todhunter School in New York City. This was a private school for girls, and Eleanor served as vice-principal and senior-class teacher of American history and English and American literature. She also gave a course called "Happenings" that dealt with current affairs. Not satisfied to have the girls discuss what they read in papers, she took them on expeditions to see for themselves. She led them into courtrooms, to police lineups, and into the slums to get a better understanding of what other people faced who were not as well off as they.

On a typical Sunday night, she rushed down the stairs of the Executive Mansion and clutched a heavy brief case filled with teaching material. She gulped a glass of milk and munched crackers as she hurried to the car that would take her to the station. She spent the next three days teaching at Todhunter. Then on Wednesday afternoon at four, she was back in the Executive Mansion as hostess at the weekly public reception. During the rest of the week there were several teas and at least one formal dinner.

Life in the Executive Mansion was a madhouse. When the children were home for holidays or weekends, they played ball in the yard, rode horses and wrestled. There was never a clear idea of who was coming to dinner. "I've laid plates for six and eighteen sat down twenty minutes later," said Eleanor. Many who came to dinner expected her to put them up overnight. But it was fun to Eleanor because Franklin was happy as governor.

Besides Todhunter, Val-Kill and her social responsibilities, she did many other things. She wrote magazine articles and had a radio program. She was also a hard-working board member on several organizations, such as the Foreign Policy Association, League of Women Voters and the Women's Trade Union League. But her most important job was the work she did for her husband.

Because of his crippled condition, she often substituted for him at fairs or on speaking engagements. "The best I can do is send Eleanor," he answered one request for a speech. One time she gave nine speeches in three days.

Part of the governor's job was to see that state prisons and reform schools and institutions for the blind, deaf, insane and aged were doing a good job. Unfortunately,

Franklin could not make the inspections himself. It was necessary that Eleanor do this for him.

On their first inspection trip they stopped outside an insane asylum. "All right," he told her, "go in and look around and let me know what is going on. Tell me how the inmates are being treated."

She returned in a little while with the day's menu. "Did you look to see whether they were actually getting this food?" he scolded her. She shook her head. "Did you bother to lift a pot cover on the stove to check whether the contents corresponded with this menu?"

"No," she said, embarrassed.

"Next time if you are going to inspect, then really inspect."

They went on to look at the state's tree shelter belt plantings. Franklin asked her to find out what they consisted of. "When I came back and described it," Eleanor admitted, "Franklin said, 'Tell me exactly what was in the first five rows. What did they plant first?' And he was so desperately disappointed when I couldn't tell him, that I put my best efforts after that into missing nothing and remembering everything."

In time she came to serve as his eyes and legs and to be his best reporter. He was proud of her. She learned to judge facial expressions, flickering eyelashes and hand motions to find out the truth. "At the institutions I inspected I learned to notice whether the beds were too close together, and whether they were folded up and put in closets or behind doors during the day. This would show that they filled the hallways at night. I also learned to watch the patients' attitude toward the staff."

When the depression came at the end of 1929 and people by the millions lost their jobs, she became a one-woman industry to lessen the suffering. Walking through Times Square in New York City, she handed out cards to the

unemployed which gave her address and said that a meal awaited them. She also bombarded people in government agencies and in private companies with requests for jobs and favors. She wrote to one friend: "This man is a carpenter but has been unable to get any work. I wonder if you would look into this and give him any possible help." The man got a job.

She took on thousands of similar cases. People at their wit's end wrote her from all over the state for help when it became known she was interested. She helped people get pensions and appeared before legislative committees to get firemen's and policemen's pensions raised. Some people tried to take advantage of her generosity. "One of my most touching and regular correspondents," she said, "was a mother whose son was in an institution. When she found I could not help her free him she begged that I go see him, which I did. Then she demanded that I go weekly and read the Bible to him!"

When Franklin was elected to a second term as governor in 1930, there were already 8,000,000 Americans unemployed. Immediately, he started a program to offer state assistance to those who were out of work in New York. Eleanor joined in the discussions of what should be done. At the same time Louis Howe, who was then working as Franklin's secretary, began laying plans to have Franklin run for the Presidency in 1932. He was then keeping up a running correspondence with 2,000 political leaders throughout the country. Eleanor, he insisted, should do the same with women politicians. As early as July, 1931, she wrote at his request to the head of the Democratic Women's Division: "I have written the enclosed letter which is to go to all women whose names are sent in to us from other states." She agreed it was now or never for Franklin.

Neither Eleanor nor Franklin went to the Democratic National Convention in Chicago in the summer of 1932. Many state delegations were supporting "favorite son" candidates, though Franklin was the single most popular candidate. Louis had gone to Chicago with James Farley, a hearty, back-slapping aide, to make certain that the various "favorite son" delegations did not combine in a "Stop Roosevelt" drive.

From his thin voice and heavy coughing when she talked

to him on the long-distance line, Eleanor was worried
about his health at the convention. Jim Farley said that
the heat and his running around to swing votes to Franklin
had reduced Louis' weight below its normal 100 pounds.
"I found him this morning racked by strangling asthma
and lying on the floor between two blowing fans," Farley
told her.

The convention fight for Franklin's nomination was not
an easy one. After three ballots, Howe and Farley had
been unable to win him the two-thirds vote he needed.
Eleanor sat up all night with Franklin listening to the
radio report of the first three ballots, which ended at 9:15
A.M. Louis called to say that things looked black for Franklin unless he agreed to accept Congressman John Garner
of Texas as his running mate for the Vice-Presidency. "If
you do it," he coughed, "your nomination is assured."
Franklin agreed. Eleanor rose immediately and took his
hand. "I am going to make some bacon and eggs for us,"
she said. And this was how they celebrated his expected
nomination.

Louis Howe was right. Franklin was nominated on the
next ballot, and Eleanor flew to Chicago with him so he
could make his acceptance speech to the convention. Immediately upon landing, she sought out Louis. She found
him frail and pale, but his wizened face was wreathed in
a smile. "I told you your husband would be President,"
he said.

"But there is still the campaign against President
Hoover," she protested.

The campaign period was hectic. There were parades
and speeches and motor escorts rushing them to audito-
riums along the route of their campaign train. She disliked
speed and noise, and her first thought in the crowded
buildings was whether there were enough fire escapes. But
she smilingly helped Franklin at every task he assigned

her. She also found time to work on two books: one, a
children's book, *When You Grow Up to Vote.* The other
was *Hunting Big Game in the Eighties,* containing many
of the letters her father wrote her during his short thirty-
four years. Her friend, the noted aviatrix Amelia Earhart,
had also begun giving her flying lessons. But Franklin put
a halt to this activity. "Eleanor, what are you trying to do
to me?" he said, annoyed. "You know I have enough worries on my mind without worrying about your flying
around up there somewhere in the sky."

On election night, Eleanor was with Franklin at his
campaign headquarters in New York City. Louis had refused to join them. Sure that this would mean bad luck for
Franklin, he went alone to his own office across the street.

At eleven P.M. when it was obvious that Franklin had
defeated Hoover, she went across the street to get him.
She found Louis hunched over pieces of papers and total-
ing the vote so far state by state. He stared silently at her
for a while. Then he opened a desk drawer and pulled out
a bottle of sherry. Carefully he poured a little into two
glasses. "I put that bottle away twenty years ago after the
fight over Blue-Eyed Billy Sheehan," he announced. "And
I vowed then that I wouldn't drink it until Franklin was
President."

Shortly after Eleanor Roosevelt returned to her husband's side, two strangers entered the room. "Yes, may I
help you?" she asked.

"We are Secret Service men," they replied. "Our job is
to guard the President."

It came over her then that the President was a prisoner
in a strong sense, guarded and watched all the time. There
would be no more easy friendships or doing what one
wanted while they lived in the White House. "I was happy
for my husband because in many ways it made up for the
blow he suffered when he was stricken with infantile

paralysis. And I had confidence in his ability to help the country in its crisis. But I knew what traditionally lay before me. The turmoil in my heart and mind was rather great that night."

She thought about this the day after the election when she returned to her class at Todhunter. The girls greeted her in awe as "First Lady."

"But I haven't changed any inside," she protested.

Chapter 9

FIRST LADY

MRS. ROOSEVELT was forty-eight when she moved into the White House. It seemed like many lifetimes ago that she had gone there to visit with Franklin when Uncle Ted was President.

Times were quiet then. But now there were 15,000,000 people unemployed and great despair throughout the country. A few days after Franklin's inauguration, she went with him to visit Oliver Wendell Holmes, the great Supreme Court justice. It was the old gentleman's ninety-second birthday and he held a book of Plato in his gnarled hands when they entered.

"You are the greatest living American," Franklin told him. "You have lived through half of our country's history. You have seen its great men. This is a dark hour, Justice Holmes. What is your advice?"

The old man's hand quivered as he stared at Eleanor and then at Franklin. "You are in a war, Mr. President. I was in a war, too—the Civil War. And in a war there is only one rule." His voice rose in volume. "Form your battalions and fight!"

Franklin nodded purposefully.

His actions were swift and dramatic. In a hundred days he turned the tide. With the help of Congress, he won passage of bills to save the banking system, give aid to farmers and home owners, reform the stock exchange and help the railroads from going bankrupt. He also started the

Civilian Conservation Corps to give a half-million young men jobs in the nation's forests; a half-billion-dollar relief program for the unemployed; a public works program to build more than three billion dollars' worth of airports, schools and post offices; the Tennessee Valley Authority; and labor laws to provide fairer working conditions and higher wages.

During all this time the White House lights burned far into the night. "The men would be working in every room," said Mrs. Roosevelt. "I could not go to bed out of personal curiosity to know what was being done."

When she first went to Washington, she quit teaching at Todhunter and turned over the Val-Kill furniture shop to the workers. She looked ahead sadly to four years of boredom in the White House. She had asked Franklin on the way down from New York if he would let her help him with the White House mail. "I won't feel so useless then," she said.

"No, you can't help on the mail, Eleanor," he said firmly. "That's my secretary's job. But you will probably have some other things to keep you busy."

Once in the White House, she concentrated on making it livable. She wanted the 16-acre estate with the 60-room house to be cozy and informal, even though Ike Hoover, Chief Usher at the White House for more than 40 years, insisted life there must be stiff and formal. When she insisted on running the elevator herself, he told her with a frown, "That just isn't done, Mrs. Roosevelt."

"It is now," she smiled back and started the controls. That first day in the White House Ike Hoover, who was no relation to former President Herbert Hoover, grew angry when he saw her pushing furniture around. The first floor of the White House was the public floor and millions of Americans came each year to inspect that level. The Presidential family lived on the second and third floors, where tourists were barred. Not only did Ike Hoover watch her hauling furniture from one upper room to another, but she also brought tourists up to see what was going on. Once she brought some grizzly Maine lobstermen through the upstairs rooms. She showed them the spot where she enjoyed her breakfast while gazing out at the magnolia tree planted by Andrew Jackson a century before. "She ain't stuck up, she ain't dressed up and she ain't afeared ter talk," one lobsterman piped up.

There were many other ways in which she made her White House living informal. Baby grandchildren could be heard crying and cooing on the upper floor by visitors on the first floor. Dogs barked and had free run of the place. Eleanor hung a rope swing from a tree on the White House lawn and sometimes tourists gaped through the iron fence at her and daughter Anna swinging double, standing up. In the morning, Eleanor would rush inside Franklin's room and deposit a few babies in bed with him. It was also a common sight for her to dictate while bouncing a child or two on her knees. Once visitors found her acting the part of a bucking bronco with one of her grandchildren hanging on to her hair for dear life. Upstairs at night her younger boys whacked each other in pillow fights and wrestled just when quiet had descended on the White House.

She also made a major overhauling of the old-fashioned and unsanitary conditions she found. The kitchen was a dark dungeon with stoves and sinks that dated back to the last century. These she modernized and replaced the cracked china which the servants were afraid to handle. All over the house, the leaky roof discolored the walls. The plumbing was so decayed that it often failed. To her disgust she found the sewer pipe to be an open trough. Worst of all, the White House was infested with rats. But in a short time, through her efforts, the residence of Presidents was brought up-to-date.

Traditionally, the wife of the President stayed far in the background. However, because of Franklin's reliance on his wife, it was impossible that she remain a smiling housekeeper and social hostess. There were too many problems going on at one time and he needed her help.

In March, 1933, when Franklin took office, 11,000 unemployed veterans of World War I marched on Washington. The year before, 20,000 had come to Washington in search of a money bonus for their war service. This earlier group had been driven from the capital with tear gas and tanks.

President Roosevelt wanted no recurrence of 1932, though the veterans were making dire threats against the Government unless something was done for them. Louis Howe had been given the job of getting them to leave town, but he made little progress. Eleanor was still moving furniture about the White House her first week there when Louis asked her to go riding with him. He directed her past the Lincoln Memorial and then he requested her to turn off the ignition.

"Louis, what is this place and what are we going to do here?" she asked.

"It's the Bonus Army." He pointed to a camp. "I want you to go into their camp. Talk to the boys. Make a tour of the place. See what they are eating and find out how they are getting along. And above all, be sure to tell them that Franklin sent you."

"But aren't you coming with me?" she stammered.

He gave her a little push out the door. "No," he barked. "I'm going to take a nap. Now get going in there and you're not to miss a thing."

She described what happened. "Very hesitatingly I got out and walked over to a lineup of men waiting for food.

They looked at me curiously and one of them asked me my name and what I wanted." In a minute word spread like wildfire that the President's wife had come to pay them a call and look into their welfare.

She went through the camp, inspected their miserable quarters, and ate with them in their eating hall. She also gave them a motherly speech and the cheers rang out when she led them in singing the old songs of World War I. After she listened to their complaints, they followed her through the mud to her car. The noise of their cheering awakened Louis. "On the way back I answered every question he put to me."

When they returned to the White House, Secret Service men met her in anger. "Don't you realize how dangerous a thing you did? They might have done something harmful to you and we would have been at fault. You should have had our protection."

"But I did have protection." She pointed to the wizened little man with her. "Mr. Howe came along to protect me."

The result of her visit to the camp was that the veterans agreed to leave Washington and return home.

Louis Howe quickly pushed her into other activities. "You must hold regular press conferences for women reporters," he told her the next day. "Half the people in this country are women and they'd be much interested in your opinions and what you do."

"But no President's wife has ever held a press conference," she argued.

"But you will," he said. "Besides, I heard that all the Washington newsladies are going to lose their jobs because publishers are trying to save money. Unless you do something all those girls will lose their means of livelihood." He smiled when she looked shocked.

She held a press conference each Thursday morning. At first she talked only about minor matters. But as time passed, she permitted the newspaperwomen to ask questions to learn her opinion on any political subject. She was nervous at first because she knew that some questions were worded to make her talk about things she shouldn't. For instance, to find out if Franklin planned to run for a second term, one woman asked, "Are you doing any thinking about what you will wear to the next Inaugural Ball?" Louis Howe taught her how to recognize such questions and to give a vague but pleasant reply in return.

One result of the press conferences she held was that she became as well known as Franklin throughout the country. But Louis Howe still was not satisfied and urged her into further activities. She began writing magazine articles. She also undertook a monthly question-and-answer column for a women's magazine, a weekly newspaper column on life in the White House, and a regular radio-broadcasting assignment. In her gentle manner, she made Franklin's activities personal to the entire country. As for the money she received for these activities plus her 100 lectures a year around the country, she turned it all over to various charities.

The busier she got, the more things she did. She was acquiring a reputation as a fighter. When she went on a tour of the wretched slums surrounding the Capitol Building, she was so shocked that she demanded that Congress do something about them. The result was the Alley Dwelling Act, a beginning to make life better for those unfortunates who lived in those neighborhoods, and to make a showplace of the Capitol area. She did a similar job for the colored Home for the Aged of Washington. The place was ready to collapse, was overrun with rats, and the inmates were not given adequate food. To a congressional committee, she pointed out, "We should be ashamed. I was sickened. If that is the way we care for people who are not able to care for themselves, we are at a pretty low ebb of civili-

zation." Not long afterward, Congress corrected this horrible situation.

Being in the news as much as she was, mail began pouring into the White House for her by the truckload. In her first nine months in the White House, she received more than 300,000 letters. More than half the writers asked for money or jobs. She sent a nine-year-old boy a banjo when he sent her a pathetic plea for one. Whenever a letter moved her, she sent a check in return. Once she sent a package of food to a woman who claimed she and her daughter were starving. The woman would not accept the package. "I want money," she scolded Mrs. Roosevelt in her next letter. A man once wrote her: "I have already wrote the President and I don't hear from you. I will write to Uncle Sam and tell him about you."

Franklin wanted her to save some of her time for him. He needed her to go out into the country and make investigations for him. He sent her that first summer to West Virginia to investigate conditions in the mining area. She went down mine shafts to see how the men worked and into miners' homes to note how poorly they lived. She went down so many mines that a popular cartoon showed two grimy miners looking up the mine shaft and exclaiming, "Here comes Mrs. Roosevelt!"

The worst spot was along Scott's Run, not far from Morgantown. Most of the miners were unemployed but had no money to move from their coal-dust-filled shacks. "There were children," Eleanor told Franklin on her return, "who did not know what it was to sit down at a table and eat a proper meal." They slept on rags on the floor.

She proposed that a model housing project be established there. She also asked that clinics and schools be built and small factories developed so that the people would not be entirely dependent on mining. Franklin did as she wished.

The West Virginia mining area trip was only the first of hundreds of places Franklin sent her. In 1934, he asked her to go to Puerto Rico and the Virgin Islands. "If you go there," he told her, "the people will know I am interested in their welfare."

She found both places poverty-stricken. "On my return," she said, "I begged my husband to send down some labor people and industrialists to look over the situation." She wanted them to draw up plans for bringing new industries to those islands and raising the standard of living. Franklin did as she suggested. But it was years before real progress began to be made.

After this trip he sent her to the Dust Bowl in the Midwest where the winds were carrying off precious topsoil and bankrupting farmers and cattlemen. He had her look into working conditions in various plants and note how minority groups were being treated in various parts of the country. Often he interrupted Cabinet Meeting discussions to say, "About that situation, my Missus told me this . . ." As soon as she returned from a trip, he would have her come immediately to his office. "Well, Babs," as he called her when they were alone, "what is the story?"

"My eyes," he referred to her proudly. He sent her on so many expeditions that sometimes he lost track of their purpose. Once he sent her out to investigate conditions in federal prisons. The rush of other business caused him to forget her errand. "Where's my Missus?" he stopped Eleanor's secretary, Malvina Thompson, one morning.

"She's in prison," Miss Thompson told him.

"I'm not surprised," Franklin laughed. "But what for?"

When she was away on these trips that averaged 40,000 miles a year, he often wrote her poetic notes. Once he wrote, "The Lord only knows when this will catch up with my Will o' the Wisp wife." Many stories appeared in print about her travels. There was one of the father telling his son the tale of Robinson Crusoe. "And there on the sand Crusoe suddenly saw two footprints. Whose do you think they were?" the father asked.

"Mrs. Roosevelt, Papa," came the reply.

In her vast travels she went chiefly by plane. At that time most people considered air travel too risky. But when they saw the First Lady flying hither and yon, the national fear disappeared. Commercial airlines happily agreed that she did more to popularize air travel than anyone else.

Besides her inspections for her husband, Eleanor influenced many of his decisions. For instance, always interested in youth, she wanted something done to keep their hope alive during the depression. Millions were too poor to finish high school or go to college. "But this is the generation that must take over after us," she argued. "If it is poorly educated the entire world will suffer."

With the help of a few government officials, she originated a program to help the country's young. She called it the National Youth Administration. Her proposed government agency would offer boys and girls part-time work to keep them in high school and college. The work would all be related to school activities, such as helping teachers and professors in running experiments, looking up references and typing exams.

"We don't feel we should talk to the President about it as yet," said the officials who helped her draw up the program. "We do not know that the country will accept it."

That night when Franklin was reading in bed, Eleanor came into the room with a serious expression on her face. "Well, well," he said, "what is bothering you?"

She described the NYA idea and told him of the fear her co-workers had expressed. "But do you think it is right to do this?" he asked.

"It will be a great help to the young people," she said. "Six million of them will get a proper education who would not otherwise. But I don't want you to do it if you think it is politically unwise."

He laid aside the report he was reading and nodded. "If you think it is the right thing to do for our young people, then it should be done." He smiled. "I guess I can stand the criticism if there is to be some."

The NYA turned out to be a political success and an enormous help to millions of young people in completing their education. "It was not as an answer—but simply as giving hope," said Mrs. Roosevelt with modesty.

If her NYA adventure did not prove controversial, many of her other activities did. There was discrimination against women in the government service and private industry, and she fought this. She called the head of one government agency to the White House for lunch one day. He had been signing contracts with private firms which paid women workers less per hour than men at the same job. "But it has always been customary to pay women less," he argued.

"A wrong is not made right by habit," she replied. The result was that he ordered all contracts changed.

When she found that government agencies employed women solely as clerks or typists, she insisted to Franklin that this must be changed. "Where are professionally trained women to go if the Government does not set the example?" she asked.

He agreed to the extent that he appointed Frances Perkins as Secretary of Labor. Madam Perkins was the first woman ever appointed to a Cabinet post. Women lawyers, economists and scientists quickly followed into government service.

Perhaps Mrs. Roosevelt's single most controversial activity was her interest in the welfare of Negroes. She served as trustee of Howard University, the excellent Negro institution in Washington, invited Negroes to the White

House, and helped many to find jobs in government and private industry. In addition, she raised money and contributed her own to build and improve schools and hospitals for them.

Most of the criticism heaped upon her for her interest in the welfare of Negroes came not because of these activities. It arose instead because of her demand that they be treated not as inferior Americans but as equals. They must have equal job and educational opportunities, she said in hundreds of speeches.

Many condemned her for her position because this would mean a revolution in the thinking in certain sections of the country. Feeling ran so strong against her in some Southern states that a few people there threatened her with physical harm or arrest if she practiced what she preached while visiting those sections. Once when in Birmingham, Alabama, she went to a meeting of whites and Negroes in a church. Negroes were seated on one side of the aisle and whites on the other. The chief of police said he would arrest her if she violated the segregation law and sat on the Negro side. It was his plan to have her sit among the whites and to take her picture there to show she was not sincere in her beliefs.

She fooled him, however. Calling for a folding chair, she set it in the aisle between both sections. Then as the police watched, she moved it closer to the Negro section. There was laughter and applause at the way she solved the problem.

So, in a short time, Eleanor Roosevelt was known as the most controversial, as well as the most active, First Lady in American history. Her friend Clare Boothe Luce described Eleanor's role: "No woman has ever so comforted the distressed or so distressed the comfortable." Those who liked her called her the conscience of America. The minority who didn't fumed at the mention of her name. "Those

Roosevelts!" they said, as if Eleanor and Franklin Roosevelt were a single person.

Indeed they were a team. He was President, and if she had been given her proper title, it would have been Assistant President. She doubled for him in handling many social activities custom set on the President's shoulders. For instance, to give him more time for his real duties, she substituted for him in laying a pile of wreaths on enough monuments to dwarf the tall Washington Monument in Washington. She also attended hundreds of dedications, received swarms of delegations on the White House lawn, and sent her congratulations to worthy organizations in every state.

Besides relieving him of such social duties, she assisted him in many other ways. She helped guide his reading by putting "interesting things on the table next to his bed." She left there summaries of reports that she thought important for him to read or use in speeches. She supplied him with names of officials whom she believed he should see. Sometimes she left him poems or novels to help him relax. Once she left him the thousand-page *Gone With the Wind*. When he returned it the next morning she was sure he could not have read this Civil War classic. "I told him so—but I couldn't catch him on a single point."

Sometimes with a purpose he took the opposite position at dinner in discussions with her on government policy. Once he made her angry by arguing against everything she said about American policy toward Great Britain. She left the table feeling like a fool. The next day he asked her to have tea with him and the American ambassador to Britain. To her shock, he ordered the ambassador to proceed in the manner she had proposed at dinner! "Without giving me a glance, he calmly stated as his own the policies he had argued against the night before!"

Oddly enough, Eleanor Roosevelt's unique role as First

Lady in no way interfered with the customary duties of that position. There was the enormous amount of entertaining required of the First Family. The formal season ran from December until Lent and included five stiffly formal dinners and five receptions. In addition each year there were dozens of other less formal receptions, at many of which Eleanor had to shake 5,000 hands and serve oceans of tea and coffee. Sometimes she had to hold two receptions the same afternoon.

With so many hands to shake, it was important to learn to do it properly. Otherwise, her hand would swell to pumpkin-size. Her formula was simple. "Don't let the line stop. Grasp the other person's hand first and draw her past you as you say, 'How do you do.' Stop every thousand hands and have a drink of water." Another important rule was "to think kindly in order to be able to have the right attitude toward people who pass by and make them feel welcome."

Even so, handshaking was a strain. Once, said Mrs. Roosevelt, "I walked into the dining room after the receiving line was over and saw two old friends. 'Where did you come from?' I asked. They told me they had gone through the line and I had shaken hands warmly."

She never realized before coming to the White House how many people want to shake the hand of the First Lady. Once when she spoke at a college, the college president asked her to shake hands with the audience before and after her talk. When she told him she would not have time for all this, he said, "If you cancel anything, I'd rather you shook hands and didn't give the lecture!"

Because of his crippled legs, Franklin found it a torture to stand in his heavy braces to receive the thousands who came to shake his and Eleanor's hands. Once he sent her a note: "Another year let's cut it out and take a trip to Samoa and Hawaii instead!" Another time while there were still about a thousand persons to take his hand, he whispered to her, "I can't stand it another minute. Another minute, I tell you."

"It will soon be over," she soothed him. "Just hold on a little longer." He smiled back weakly, but held his place until the last hand was shaken.

If there was good news in her husband's first term, there was also bad. Louis Howe was swiftly running downhill. Franklin had made him his chief assistant when he became President. When the Governor of Kentucky named him an honorary colonel, Louis handed Eleanor the new calling card he had printed. It read, COL. LOUIS RASPUTIN VOL-TAIRE TALLEYRAND SIMON LEGREE HOWE. Franklin's and her devotion to their little friend was full.

It was in the fall of 1934 that Louis' health slipped noticeably. Eleanor insisted that he cut down on his work. His breathing came so hard now that he could not walk a block. When he returned to Washington from a trip, Eleanor arranged with train porters to ride him through the station on a luggage cart. She watched him struggle to stay alive and his weakness saddened her days. Yet his spirit never lessened. "I've been as close to Franklin as his valet," he told her when he was confined to a bed in the White House, "and he is still a hero to me."

He lived a year and a half with his wasted body, but his eyes shone bright. For several months Eleanor nursed him, but in April, 1936, he died. *Devoted friend, adviser and associate of the President* was written on his tombstone. "And of Eleanor Roosevelt," it might have been added.

There was little time to mourn, for Franklin had announced he would run for a second term. Eleanor was in the midst of this campaign, though she did so without publicity. She worked to reorganize the Democratic Party's campaign program, and wrote a long report for her husband that became the Bible of the 1936 campaign. She also made rules of behavior for herself on campaign trips she took with Franklin: "Always be on time. Do as little talking as humanly possible. Never let yourself be disturbed by anything. Always do whatever you are told as quickly as possible. Remember to lean back in the parade car so everybody can see the President. Be sure not to get too fat, because you'll have to sit three in the back seat."

The election was one of the most lopsided in American history. She watched her husband carry every state except Maine and Vermont. "But we lost the village of Hyde Park," she reminded him laughingly.

During the next four years, Eleanor stepped up her pace, which amazed Franklin. She expanded her investigations, her lectures, her writing. She began a daily newspaper column called *My Day*. At first her column was a record of how she spent each day. Later on she began expressing her opinion on all subjects. Some people found it indecent that any woman, let alone the wife of the President, would express her views in print. Other people thought it gave her husband an unfair political advantage to have such an active and outspoken wife.

Her column created a real problem at first because it had to be sandwiched among all her other heavy activities. Yet somehow she went to press every day. Sometimes she dictated her column with a grandchild on her lap and pulling her hair; sometimes while sitting on a rock on top of a mountain; sometimes in a speeding car, or a hotel bed or on a destroyer. Once while dictating in her bath, the water ran over.

One thing Eleanor tried to do during Franklin's second term was to bring him a wide assortment of guests to relax him at dinner. She brought him ministers, explorers, social workers, editors, writers, artists, musicians, professors and doctors. Many were invited simply to entertain him. Carl

Sandburg came one time, strummed his guitar, sang some folk songs and refreshed Franklin.

Sometimes Eleanor was so busy that she was unable to be present for dinner. Her little black appointment book was crowded with as many as 20 appointments for a single day. One day she visited a rural housing project and made 14 speeches. She was not the sort to travel about in a chauffeured limousine. In New York she rode the subway and the Fifth Avenue bus. People were shocked to discover the First Lady holding on to a subway strap. In department stores she rode up and down the regular elevators. Once a woman who had been staring at her said, "But you can't be Mrs. Roosevelt. She would never do this." She smiled and told her it was.

She rode the elevators because she had so many presents to buy for people. She kept a large card-index file of persons to whom she sent Thanksgiving, Christmas, birthday, wedding and anniversary presents. On birthdays, she not only sent a cake but also the candles. Overnight guests at the White House were surprised when handed a box lunch before leaving in the morning. At Thanksgiving, she sent out hundreds of boxes of "goodies" for homes of friends throughout the country. Once a man wrote her that he expected a turkey instead of the capon she sent him! The weeks before Christmas she was up past two A.M. packaging a ton of candy to be sent out.

"How does she do all these things without collapsing?" people asked in amazement. "It is simple," a relative admitted. "The Roosevelts were born with an extra gland."

But it was not only her great energy that carried her along. It was the training she had had from her father and Mlle. Souvestre, her old teacher. There was satisfaction in life only in helping others less fortunate; and there were so many in this position then. Her life was dedicated to unselfish service for others. It was her duty to do so. And because she was in such an exceptional position as First Lady, her duty was larger than that of others.

It was her energy, sense of duty and ability that made her the most powerful woman in the world during Franklin's terms in office. The editors of *Time* described her as "a woman of unequaled influence in the world, but unlike Cleopatra, the great Elizabeth, Pompadour, or Catherine of Russia, her power is not that of a ruler. She is the wife of a ruler but her power comes not from her influence on him but on public opinion."

Chapter 10

WAR AND DEATH

BY 1939, the remains of the economic depression were overshadowed by something more disturbing. Adolf Hitler, the dictator of Germany, was on the march to conquer the world. He ranted about Germans as a "master" race with the destiny of enslaving "inferior" peoples. He had already swallowed Austria and Czechoslovakia and was now making menacing motions toward Poland. One by one, Hitler hoped to divide and conquer the remaining nations of the Free World.

There was great fear throughout the world of the might of the German war machine. After coming through the slaughter of World War I and the worst of the economic depression, people craved peace. In the United States, most people were reluctant to join the remaining free nations and show unity against Hitler. Some said that any strengthening of the armed forces would only anger Hitler and make him more aggressive. Others said he should be permitted to take what countries he wanted. The Atlantic Ocean was wide enough to keep him from invading or bombing the United States. We must isolate ourselves from the rest of the world, they cried.

Over the opposition of President Roosevelt, Congress during the thirties passed neutrality laws. These said that the United States would not give aid to countries attacked by aggressors. For his opposition, Franklin Roosevelt was called a "warmonger" by those who feared Hitler.

Eleanor Roosevelt was one who believed that a strong

America and a united Free World might make Hitler think twice. She hated war, but, said she, we were morally bound to oppose aggression and slavery. To this end, she began making speeches all over the country to rally the people to take a strong stand against Hitler and his goals.

"It is not good for a nation when the wife enters the political china shop," Joseph Goebbels, Hitler's propaganda chief, screamed. Mussolini, the Italian dictator, asked the American people to "declare an embargo on Mrs. Roosevelt."

Actually, at the first meetings she addressed on foreign policy she was booed. But she continued with her talks all through 1939. Gradually her speeches began to have an effect. In time, she whipped up strong public support for her position. One editor said of her talks, "In the last six months, she did much to wean the country away from isolationism."

She agreed with Franklin that he must do something colorful to show American solidarity with free nations menaced by Hitler. To this end he invited King George VI and Queen Elizabeth of Great Britain to visit the United States in June, 1939. Great newspaper coverage was given this event. Yet typically, Eleanor was late to Union Station to greet the royal couple when they arrived in Washington. Her explanation was that she had found a family of sharecroppers stranded on a highway in the Midwest and had brought them to Washington to help them. It was in the midst of her conversation with these sharecroppers in one of the fancy White House rooms that word reached her of the arrival of the gold-and-silver-trimmed royal train.

The visit of the king and queen was a joyous success. As gracious host and hostess, Franklin and Eleanor did much to build good will in this country for England. The royal couple in turn proved to be friendly and democratic.

Besides a stay in the White House, the king and queen stayed at the Hyde Park mansion of Franklin's mother. Here Eleanor treated them to a typical American picnic complete with hot dogs and potato salad. There were several amusing accidents that Eleanor described in her *My Day* columns. Once the butler misjudged the stairs, dropped his heavy tray with a crash and came sliding on his back all the way across the library floor. Another time, the table laden with dinner collapsed. At the picnic Franklin, emphasizing a story, swept a tray of glasses into bits.

But even as they picnicked, across the ocean Hitler was making threatening gestures toward England. When the visit ended, Eleanor and Franklin took the royal couple to the little Hyde Park station. "One thought of the clouds that hung over them and the worries they were going to face," said Eleanor, "and we turned away and left the scene with a heavy heart."

Nothing could stop Hitler. He arranged an agreement with his fellow dictator, Joseph Stalin of Communist Russia. Then the German army invaded Poland. As allies of Poland, Britain and France entered the war against Germany. Eleanor was at Hyde Park on September first when Franklin called her from the White House at five A.M. "It's happened, Babs," he said huskily. "Germany has invaded Poland."

She hoped that the war would not spread. War—and she had four eligible sons, in case the United States became directly involved. "I hope we can avoid it," Franklin said.

He succeeded in getting Congress to change the neutrality acts, so that the United States could help countries under attack. But things went badly for the democracies. Hitler and Stalin gobbled Poland within weeks. Japan was devastating China. By mid-1940, Hitler's forces had overrun France, Norway, Denmark, Holland and Belgium.

England, standing alone, suffered continual air attacks and bombardment.

It was the war that made Franklin decide to run for a third term as President. No other President before him had ever held more than two terms. Eleanor was opposed to his running again. She felt that he had done his part and had earned a rest from the heavy duties of that high office. She sent him a note before he made up his mind: "You know I do not believe in it." But in the end she had to admit there was no other leader among the Democrats who could inspire the American people as Franklin could.

A spontaneous movement arose in late spring of 1940 to have her run for President. A national poll revealed that she was even more popular than her husband. But she quickly said she would not.

There was no problem in Franklin's winning the nomination from the Democratic National Convention that summer. Delegates cheered his name wildly. But when he requested that the convention name Henry Wallace, the Secretary of Agriculture, as the party's Vice-Presidential nominee, delegates rebelled. Wallace was not a professional politician, nor did they know much about him, convention leaders claimed.

For a time it looked as though the convention would collapse in name-calling over Wallace. Delegates booed his name and marched about the hall protesting his candidacy. Finally James Farley, Franklin's convention manager, called Eleanor. "You've got to come to Chicago," he pleaded. "We need you—badly."

"I'll fly out tomorrow," she told him reluctantly. She had never taken part in a national convention and did not know if professional politicians would welcome her.

"The delegates are in an ugly mood," Farley warned her when he met her at the airport the next day. "It may be too late to bring order to the convention."

Even outside the convention hall she could hear the booing. Inside, she watched delegates running about amid confusion. Finally, she climbed unnoticed onto the platform. A politician hurried to her and said with desperation, "This is the time for you to speak."

Tall and erect, she walked to the speaker's stand. Spotlights blinded her and the odor of stale cigar smoke hung in the air. Suddenly the delegates caught sight of her standing there. They hurried back to their seats. Complete silence followed. Not a cough or a chair squeak was heard during her short talk. It was her great dignity more than her words that brought the delegates to their senses. She talked about the burdens of the Presidency, how Franklin thought that Wallace would best carry out his foreign policy should anything happen to him during the third term. She told the delegates that they must bury political differences and concentrate on doing "what this country can to bring this world to a safer and happier condition."

At her conclusion there was no applause. "I felt as though I was in church," one delegate said. The organist began playing "God Bless America," and when he finished she took her seat. Then began the applause which lasted several minutes. With little trouble Wallace was now nominated for Vice-President. Convention leaders agreed that her speech had saved the day for Franklin.

As soon as the Wallace nomination was completed, she drove to the airport and caught a commercial plane for home. The plane was already down the runway when the call came for it to return to its starting place. There was a phone call for Mrs. Roosevelt, someone shouted. It was the President of the United States. "I want to thank you, Babs," Franklin said. "You did a very good job. God bless you."

Once the election against Wendell Willkie (whom Eleanor admired) was won, Franklin could now devote himself to the sad international situation. The year 1941 saw a big build-up of American war industries and the armed forces. When Russia was attacked by Germany that June, Franklin added aid to her as well as to Britain and China. Franklin selected Harry Hopkins, the Government's relief administrator, to act as go-between for him with foreign nations. Eleanor was given the task of keeping him in touch with developments within the country. The *Wall Street Journal* said of her: "Watch her for tips on policies . . . She talks to officials . . . has been calling on bigwigs . . ."

All year long the country worked feverishly to make up for lost time. The "arsenal of Democracy," Franklin labeled the United States. From state to state, Eleanor traveled to raise factory morale and to see that women workers and Negroes were treated fairly. She also inspected army camps for Franklin and christened ships.

In the midst of all these activities two tragedies occurred. Both Franklin's mother and Eleanor's brother Hall died during the month of September. The old lady, then 86, had mellowed and was fiercely proud at the end that her son had overcome his physical disability to lead the nation. As for Eleanor, she had been close to her six-foot, three-inch yellow-haired giant of a brother and the loss was a shock to her.

War came suddenly and with unexpected fury to the United States on December 7, 1941, with the Japanese attack on Pearl Harbor. By agreement, Germany and Italy also declared war on the United States a few days later. It was time now to concentrate on survival and on the world's future.

With the Pearl Harbor attack, the West Coast suffered from hysteria and feared a Japanese invasion. Some people said that spies had already landed. At Franklin's request, Eleanor spent a week traveling up and down the coast. She made speeches and walked about fearlessly to calm the rattled population. For a short time, she also became the assistant head of the Office of Civilian Defense. This was the only official government position she took while Franklin was President. Here working without pay, her job was to set up a program for bomb shelters, emergency medical aid and ways to bolster civilian morale.

She found she had to be cautious about what she said. For instance, early in 1942, she spoke over the radio and urged housewives to cut down on their use of sugar because the supply was limited. Early the next morning across the nation a wild stampede of housewives cleaned out grocery stores of sugar. After this she was doubly careful what she said.

To spur production, she joined Franklin on long inspection trips of factories producing war supplies. Such trips had to be kept secret because the country was at war. Workers were surprised to look up from their assembly lines and find the Presidential jeep coasting by. "If it ain't old Frank and Eleanor!" a worker once shouted as they approached him. Franklin had acquired a little black Scottie named Fala, who went along on these trips. "The Informer," the Secret Service named Fala because he had to be walked several times a day and was easily recognized.

The war was going badly in both the European and Asiatic sectors in 1942. The result was that Eleanor stepped up her visits to war plants to plead with workers to produce more. There were military hospitals to visit now, too, with the casualty rate on the increase. In addition, family life was disrupted with so many mothers taking jobs in war plants. Franklin asked Eleanor to suggest programs to him to save the family institution and curtail the rising juvenile delinquency. She also plunged into the problems of service people and their dependents. Many a hardship case she handled personally. When she couldn't, she asked for help from responsible officials. On one of her requests, Franklin wrote to the Under Secretary of War, "What shall I tell Mrs. Roosevelt about this?"

In order not to take advantage of her position, she eliminated fancy foods at the White House and cut individual portions. This created a problem because so many wartime guests came. When Washington hotels grew crowded, she filled various rooms and hallways in the White House with cots for servicemen passing through town.

One frequent visitor was Winston Churchill, Britain's Prime Minister. Churchill came to work with Franklin on war strategy and the postwar. "They used to argue on military tactics all the time," said Eleanor. Without any false formality, Mrs. Roosevelt and the Prime Minister treated each other like family members. Once when she, Churchill, Harry Hopkins and Franklin went for a ride, she wanted to sit in the front seat. Churchill insisted that she ride in back with Franklin. When she argued, said Churchill, "the British Empire went into action. After about three minutes' conflict of wills, I won and we whirled off amid our cyclist escort."

Madame Chiang Kai-shek was another visitor, as was Foreign Minister Molotov of the Soviet Union. Molotov brought along a suitcase filled with dark rye bread, a salami and a loaded pistol. "I heard that the White House food was considered poor," Eleanor laughed, "but I didn't realize our food was that bad." Eleanor also enjoyed a close relationship with Norway's Crown Princess Martha and her children, and the royal family of Holland. The old Queen Wilhelmina was one of Eleanor's favorites and she once took her to her press conference. Wilhelmina's daughter, Juliana, was like a daughter to Eleanor and she became the godmother of one of Juliana's daughters.

Although entertaining foreign visitors became big business during the war, Eleanor did not let this interfere with her many other activities. Once Franklin found she had stayed up all night answering mail after an evening of entertaining, and he scolded her. Another time when Churchill came she fell asleep at the dinner table. The Prime Minister, a noted talker, was sure it was his conversation. He was hurt until he learned she had spent eight hours that day at the Office of Civilian Defense, plus writing her column and attending three social functions.

When England underwent ceaseless air bombardment in 1942, Franklin asked her to fly there in October. "Your visit will do much to raise the spirits of the British people," he told her. "Besides, we are going to invade North Africa soon and I think it would be good timing if you talked to our troops before they leave England."

No announcement was made of her crossing. Yet an enormous crowd was on hand at London's Paddington Station when her train arrived on October 23. The king and queen were there to greet her, as were General Eisenhower and British Foreign Secretary Anthony Eden. The headline on the *Daily Mirror* read: WE'RE SURE GLAD TO HAVE YOU MA'AM!

She stayed with the king and queen at Buckingham Palace for two days. Then she was off on a three-week dash through army camps, factories, shipyards and bomb-devastated areas. Franklin had given her the security name of "Rover," which fitted her well. Once when she set out to visit an air force camp where her son Elliott was stationed, she lost her way. The security call for directions to the American Embassy in London read: *Rover has lost her pup.*

Despite a bad cold, she would not ease her crowded schedule. "You'll never make it, Mrs. Roosevelt," an old friend scolded her. But he was wrong. She was a blur as she rushed from camp to camp, pausing for talks with individual soldiers. Franklin had asked her to note their complaints so he could correct them. They needed thicker socks. The folks back home were writing them sad letters about how they were suffering from sugar, coffee, meat and tire shortages. Everywhere she collected family addresses back in the States and promised to write and call the families on her return.

She made inspections in heavy downpours without rubbers or raincoat. She wanted to see as much as she could. Mrs. Churchill traveled with her a short time until she collapsed on a stairway from exhaustion. Eleanor had a genuine touch with people. Once when she talked to fire wardens, whose job it was to extinguish fires caused by incendiary bombs, one warden wiped his eyes afterward and mumbled, "She tried to make a blinkin' 'ero of me."

But after three weeks of such travels, Franklin wanted her home. I DON'T CARE HOW YOU SEND HER, he wired the American Embassy. JUST SEND HER. Churchill was reluctant to see her go. He wrote her later, "Your visit has given great pleasure and comfort throughout this island and y^r presence and speeches have been an inspiration to the many places you have visited in y^r indefatigable tour. . . . You certainly have left golden footprints behind you."

With this success behind her, Franklin asked her to make a similar trip to the South Pacific in 1943. "The boys out there haven't had many visitors," he told her, "and you'll do them a lot of good."

This trip was another amazing exhibition of energy and endurance. She flew 23,145 miles and made 17 island stops. In New Zealand she covered 1,000 miles in old trains, and on the islands she bumped along jungle roads in jeeps and command cars. There were hospitals filled with wounded to visit, camps to inspect and outposts manned by lonely soldiers. Fighting in the Pacific had been especially heavy.

It was a rough trip for a woman nearing sixty. Besides having the war close by, there were other dangers. On one island when she turned on the light in her room, she found the floor crawling with red bugs. "I nearly disgraced myself with screaming," she admitted. She visited Guadalcanal where the fighting was costly. Franklin had written the admiral in charge that she was not to go there. But she insisted and the admiral gave in. Everywhere she went, as in England, she told soldiers she would deliver messages to their families. One soldier wrote home, "I have always been agin' her until now, but she has the faculty of seeming as though she is not in the slightest hurry, that she came all the way out here just to talk to you and you and you." When Franklin heard that she was considering a delay in returning, he said, "Oh, Lord, make Eleanor tired."

She was tired, too, when she returned. She had lost 30 pounds and during her last week in the jungles, she had gone about with a case of pneumonia. Yet rather than rest when she was back in Washington, she began immediately to get in touch with the families of the soldiers she had seen. Once she called a girl to tell her she had seen her husband. She did not tell the girl who she was. "Perhaps you will have lunch with me tomorrow so I can tell you all about him," she said.

"How will I recognize you?" the girl asked.

"Just look for a tall, gray-haired lady in the hotel lobby," Mrs. Roosevelt said quickly.

"Oh, no! It can't be!" the girl cried out in shock the next day when she found she was to lunch with the First Lady.

Eleanor was not the only member of the First Family to go on wartime trips. Her four boys were with the Marines, Navy and Air Force and were in the thick of the fighting. As for her husband, Franklin made several trips abroad to meet with Churchill, Stalin and Chiang Kai-shek, the Chinese leader. Some of these conferences dealt with war strategy. At others, Franklin took up his dream of creating a postwar international organization where countries could discuss their problems, get economic aid to improve standards of living, and join together to prevent war.

When he returned from the Teheran Conference early

in 1944, Eleanor noted that he suffered from a low-grade fever and a persistent cough. "You are working too hard," she told him. "You must take things easier for a while."

"But I can't," he told her wearily. "There is so much to do." He had been working day and night to plan the invasion of Europe. Problems were arising everywhere, and he had to supply the answers. All the decisions were his. So was it his responsibility for millions of American boys.

When his cough hung on, she tried in vain to cut his daily list of visitors. For she was now worried for the first time about his health. "Don't press him and wear him out," she stood outside his office and told officials who came to see him. "Go easy on him."

Fortunately, he agreed to her suggestion that he spend two weeks in April at Hobcaw, the South Carolina plantation owned by their friend Bernard Baruch. When he returned to the White House, he seemed like the Franklin of old.

By D-Day on June sixth, she noticed that he seemed full of vitality, though highly nervous and worried about the Normandy Invasion. "What are you thinking of?" she asked him. She visualized him thinking about the great fleets near the beaches and the umbrellas of airplanes meeting with Hitler's military machine.

"I wonder how Linaka will come out," he said. Russel Linaka was their Hyde Park gardener who was now in the Navy.

The year 1944 was also another election year. "All that is within me cries to go back to my home on the Hudson," he told the nation. Would he run for a fourth term? people asked. He was like an institution. Many young people could not remember another President during their lifetime. But he was tired, so tired, that Eleanor was frightened. Nonetheless, she did not protest when he told her he would run for a fourth term. "I have as little right to

withdraw as the soldier has to leave his post on the line."
Not only did he want to finish the wartime job he had
taken on, he told her, but he was the father of the United
Nations idea and he wanted to be on hand to get that
organization under way when war ended.

She was glad he did little campaigning that fall. In the
midst of it, she went with him to Quebec, Canada, to meet
with Churchill. The war was moving swiftly to a finish
in Europe and the conference dealt with what to do with
the defeated enemy. Afterward, Churchill returned with
them to Hyde Park for a few days of relaxation. They were
sitting by the fireplace, Eleanor knitting a sweater and
discussing the postwar with the two men. She said that
India must be independent of England once the war was
over. Franklin agreed with her. She watched Churchill
rise slowly, a puckish expression on his face. He pretended
to be carrying a heavy load in his arms and dropped it on
Franklin. "Do you want India?" he asked. "Here it is."

She passed her sixtieth birthday as the campaign neared
its climax in October. On the twenty-first, she joined
Franklin in an open-car ride through New York City.
More than a million people turned out to see them, even
though the rainfall that day was one of New York's heavi-
est. The last day of the campaign she was with him when
he insisted they spend that day in the district where he
had first campaigned in 1910. Memories poured out for
her as they rode from town to town. Everywhere in the
crowds surrounding their car, she seemed to find the face
of their old friend Louis Howe. Franklin even wore his
old fedora hat he had worn in 1910 and he waved it to
each crowd. He laughed and joked, but she saw now that
he looked frail and ill.

Right after his fourth-term victory, she realized that his
health had gone further downhill. When he insisted that
all their grandchildren come spend Christmas with them

in the White House, she felt he wanted to see them one last time.

After he was inaugurated for the fourth time as President in January 1945, Franklin told her that he was going to Yalta to meet with Churchill and Stalin. "We will be going over the last steps to establish the United Nations," he said with satisfaction.

"I want to go with you to Russia," she said. She wanted to be there to look after him.

"No." He shook his head. "If you go, they will all feel that they have to make a big fuss over you. No other wives will be there."

From Malta on his way home, he wrote her, "Dearest Babs: Got in safely. Lots of sleep but still need more!" She was frightened by his appearance when he finally arrived home. At their fortieth wedding anniversary on March 17, he told her, "Well, the war is almost over in Europe and it shouldn't last too long in Asia. After the war is over you and I will go to the Near East and settle the differences there. There are lots of difficulties there."

"I thought we were going home to Hyde Park?" she asked.

He ignored her interruption. "And then we'll go to the Far East." His eyes grew wide. "We'll go to China and fix things there."

"Let's go to Hyde Park," she pleaded.

He stared at her a while, and then smiled in agreement.

Each day now she found him looking worse. She prayed that he would somehow regain his health. The opening meeting to establish the United Nations was set for April 25 in San Francisco. "You and I will be there," he said. Then they would go to London and visit England. Prime Minister Churchill had announced that they would get "the biggest reception since Lord Nelson made his triumphant return to London."

But first, said Franklin to her, he wanted to go to his beloved Warm Springs for a short rest. He wanted her to remain at the White House to look after certain matters for him. Then when he returned they would head for San Francisco.

His reports from Warm Springs were all heartening. On April 12, Eleanor Roosevelt attended an afternoon charity function at the Sulgrave Club in Washington. She was sitting next to Mrs. Woodrow Wilson, the widow of the World War I President, when she was told she was wanted on the phone. Stephen Early, Franklin's press secretary, was on the other end of the line and was greatly upset.

"He asked me to come home at once. I did not even ask why." It must be that Franklin was gone, she told herself in pain. Franklin must be gone, she repeated on the ride back to the White House, as she sat with clenched fists. She thought of the boy who bounced her on his back when she was two; the boy of 16 who saved her from disgrace at a party by asking her to dance; the young and righteous man who fought "Blue-Eyed Billy" Sheehan's nomination to the Senate.

Stephen Early's eyes were wet when she arrived at the White House. What she had guessed was so. "The President has died," Early said. "But I am more sorry for the people of the country and the world than I am for us."

Her mind went blank. "I'll call Vice-President Truman," he told her.

It was the worst moment of her life. She tried to pull herself together by the time Harry Truman arrived. When he walked in, she felt her body quivering. "The President has passed away," she tried to control her voice. "He died like a soldier."

Mr. Truman choked. "What can I do?" he asked her.

"Tell us what we can do," she said to the new President. "Is there any way we can help you?"

Later she cabled her sons far away in the fighting
FATHER SLEPT AWAY. HE WOULD EXPECT YOU TO CARRY ON
AND FINISH YOUR JOBS.

That evening she flew to Warm Springs. The next day
she began the journey to bring Franklin home to rest in
Hyde Park. The polio patients at the Warm Springs
Foundation lined up to say farewell to Franklin. Their
eyes told her they had cried all night. A voice from the
crowd cried out, "Please God, take care of him."

On the train back to Washington, said Eleanor, "I lay
in my berth all night with the window shade up, looking
out at the countryside he had loved and watching the
faces of the people at stations, and even the crossroads
who came to pay their last tribute all through the night."

After Franklin was buried in his rose garden at Hyde
Park, Mrs. Roosevelt returned to the White House to re-
move the Roosevelt belongings of more than twelve years.
About 100,000 letters of condolence were there for her.
Working furiously to keep her mind off her loss, it took
her only a week before she was packed and ready to turn
the White House over to the Trumans.

On the last evening, she put on her hat and coat and
walked out the front door. In a drizzling rain, she rode to
Union Station. When she arrived in New York a private
citizen, she was surprised to find reporters crowding the
station. She shook her head when they asked for an inter-
view. "The story is over," she said, walking swiftly through
them.

Chapter 11

ON HER OWN

It was Eleanor Roosevelt's hope, after Franklin's death, that she would live out her few remaining years quietly at Hyde Park.

However, she was badly mistaken. She could have had the New York Democratic Party's nomination for United States Senator. But she turned it down. "I feel very strongly that running for office is not the way in which I can be most useful," she rejected the offer. Nevertheless, she did not turn down President Truman's plea that she become the American delegate to the newly established United Nations. "Your country needs you—indeed, this troubled world needs you," Mr. Truman wrote her. "I want to thank you," she replied, "for the opportunity you have given me of being part of this delegation. It is a great privilege and my only fear is that I shall not be able to make much of a contribution."

The London organizational meeting of the United Nations General Assembly was set for January 1946. Amid newsreel cameras and microphones, the other members of the American delegation came on board the *Queen Elizabeth* docked in New York on New Year's Eve. While they made short speeches, a taxicab rode onto the pier and a tall gray-haired woman dressed in mourning black climbed out and hurried up the gangplank. It wasn't until she was almost on board that a customs official spied her. "But Mrs. Roosevelt," he cried. "Can't I help you on board?"

During the crossing, members of the American delega-

tion met daily for discussion. There were piles of reports
for each delegate to read afterward. "I hope the United
Nations will discuss and act on problems and not bury
them," she warned the delegates.

London was curious about her. Great crowds blocked
traffic about the entrance to her hotel. They cheered themselves hoarse every time she showed her face. Men raised
their hats when she walked by and women applauded.
When the king and queen asked her to lunch at the
palace, she said, "I can't stay long because I have to get
back to work."

At the UN General Assembly session she tried to remain
in the background. However, Belgium's Prime Minister
Paul Henry Spaak, who was elected General Assembly
President, stood on the platform and pointed to her. "I
want to give a special welcome to one of the delegates,"
he beamed while she blushed. "I refer to the lady who
bears the most illustrious and respected of all names. I do
not think it would be possible to open this assembly without mentioning her." She did not dare acknowledge his
greeting, for her eyes were filled with tears.

The Assembly soon plunged into men's work. Committees were appointed and Mrs. Roosevelt was assigned
to the Social, Humanitarian and Cultural Committee. William L. White, an editor of the *Reader's Digest,* wrote
about her: "All the feeble folk—the lame, the halt, the
blind, the persecuted and despised of men, the various
minorities laboring under discrimination—all of these come
to her with their troubles as children to a mother."

The days turned into weeks of debate. The Soviet Union,
which had been a wartime ally, now showed its true colors.
Soviet delegates burst out with one wild charge after another against the West. Bewildered delegates from other
countries, who at the start considered her as a sort of
marble statue, slowly turned to Mrs. Roosevelt for advice

and guidance under this attack. "She simply moved in as a super-mother," said one observer, "presiding over a large family of often noisy, sometimes unruly, boys."

An explosion came near the end of the first Assembly's work. More than a million refugees from Poland, the Baltic States and Yugoslavia were in wretched camps in parts of Germany controlled by the United States, Britain and France. These refugees did not want to return to their homelands because they were now under Communist control. But Andrei Vishinsky, the chief Soviet delegate, demanded that they be returned regardless of their desire. Death faced them if they were sent back.

Many delegates feared that unless they did as Vishinsky demanded, the United Nations might fall apart before it really began. Hour by hour Vishinsky's threats became stronger. Throughout it all, Mrs. Roosevelt sat staring at him sternly, her anger kindling. Suddenly she rose. Her words came out softly but firmly. "We here in the United Nations," she said with great feeling, "are trying to frame things which will consider first the rights of man and what makes men more free—not governments but man!" She went on from there to demolish Vishinsky's position. John Foster Dulles, then an alternate American delegate and later Secretary of State, called her contest with Vishinsky, "One of the most dramatic episodes of the conference. Mrs. Roosevelt, with moving simplicity, pleaded for tolerance, and Mr. Vishinsky denounced tolerance as a dangerous weakness."

The delegates voted down Vishinsky's proposal. Her moving words affected the lives of more than a million persons.

She served on the American delegation to the UN for seven years, resigning at the end of 1952. When the UN moved permanently to New York, the first day she reported she was stopped by a cleaning woman. "Excuse me,

Mrs. Roosevelt," she greeted her. "I just wanted to say welcome and to tell you how glad I am to see you here. We women have a real stake in working for peace."

In all her seven years with the UN, Mrs. Roosevelt was its chief tourist attraction and most popular and effective member. Visitors queued up in long lines to catch a glimpse of her. She put in a nine A.M. to seven-thirty P.M. six-day week. There were daily meetings of the American delegation plus her committee meetings.

During all this time, the Communists considered her their worst UN enemy. The *Literary Gazette* of the Soviet Union referred to her as "a garrulous, feeble old woman consumed with an anti-Soviet fever and playing an ugly role." *Izvestia* called her "a fly darkening the Soviet sun." But such names did not bother her.

Her chief activity at the UN was the writing and passing of the document known as the Declaration of Human Rights. Because of Soviet opposition, her struggle to win UN approval of the Declaration took two years. They hampered her at every turn in her duty as chairman of the Commission on Human Rights. "Soviet delegates don't speak as free people at all," she told them frankly. "They just say what they have been ordered to say and that is all. If they ever did give signs of acknowledging a point, they wouldn't last long."

Once a Soviet delegate made a long speech saying that workers were dying of starvation in California by the thousands. "Now Mr. Pavlov has been in the United States a long time," she said when he finished. "He doesn't believe what he said. He knows better. But he was told what to say and he said it." Pavlov stared wide-eyed.

The Communists fought over every word in the Declaration as it was being written. They also had a bagful of other tricks. One was to keep a meeting going until others got tired and left the business undone. Once when they tried that, she told other members of her committee that they must outlast the Communists. Talking all day to prevent a vote on a minor point, the Reds were surprised to find all members present when evening came. "Go on," Mrs. Roosevelt urged them. Midnight passed and they grew hoarser by the minute. Patiently she continued to smile. At daybreak their voices failed entirely. "Now we will take the vote," she told them firmly, and she did.

Soviet delegates did everything they could to infuriate her. Only once did she bang her gavel in anger. "I am sorry, sir," she snapped at a Communist. "This is no place for propaganda speeches and I must ask you to draw your remarks to a close." President Truman wrote her, "I have marveled at the poise and patience that you have maintained in the face of the maddening technique of the Russians. I have observed with great satisfaction that you have put them in their place more than once."

There was one important session of her Human Rights Commission in Geneva, Switzerland. The meetings had been going on for a year now. It was already December and she warned the delegates, "I certainly intend to get back to see my sixteen grandchildren at Hyde Park for Christmas. What I propose is that only a single person will be permitted to defend or attack any point or amendment. Besides, speeches must be short."

"Dictator!" a Soviet delegate yelled. But he was voted down. For the next fourteen days she worked the commission hard. When the meetings finally ended, a red-eyed, pale Soviet delegate tottered over to her. Throughout the meetings he had denounced the West as "decadent democracies." He shook her hand and said, "Mrs. Roosevelt, you must be exhausted. I know I am and so is my wife, even though she isn't a member of the commission."

With a twinkling smile, she said, "I never felt better.

Perhaps it's because I belong to one of those 'decadent democracies.' "

The Declaration of Human Rights came up for final decision at the Paris UN session in December, 1948. The Palais de Chaillot was jammed to capacity with excited onlookers. Nor were they to be disappointed when she and her old antagonist, Andrei Vishinsky, carried out a sharp, running debate. He submitted a long series of amendments to her Declaration, in case he lost out in his demand for a year's postponement of a vote.

For two days she met every Soviet challenge. Finally on the night of December 10, Dr. Herbert V. Evatt, the General Assembly President, called for the vote. The air was electric as the first nation was called. Vishinsky sat slumped in his seat when the vote was in favor of the Declaration. When the final vote was tallied, the Soviet bloc abstained from voting to save face. "Forty-eight to nothing," Evatt announced.

All eyes turned toward her. "It is particularly fitting," Evatt said happily, "that there should be present on this occasion the person who, with the assistance of many others, has played a leading role in the work, a person who has raised to greater heights even so great a name—Mrs. Roosevelt, the representative of the United States."

The Declaration of Human Rights was merely a statement of 30 rights to which each human being was entitled. No government was legally obligated by the UN action to see to it that these rights were observed within its borders. It had only moral force. Yet the Declaration has influenced the constitutions of Costa Rica, Indonesia, India and Libya. Mrs. Roosevelt spent four fruitless years after the Declaration passed to get the non-democracies to accept it as part of their laws.

Her light brown hair was completely gray and she had become a great-grandmother by the time she quit the UN

at the close of 1952. It was now time, her children argued,
for her to sit back and take things easy. But as Admiral
Richard Byrd, her close friend for decades, wrote her, "I
don't believe you would be happy if your life were not
hectic."

The history of Eleanor Roosevelt as she moved into her
seventies showed her as busy as ever. She was writing a
daily newspaper and a monthly magazine column, writing
a half-dozen books, appearing on her own daily radio show
and weekly half-hour television program, lecturing at col-
leges and organizations, speaking before political conven-
tions, running various charities, helping individuals, and
traveling to the ends of the earth to investigate conditions
first-hand and advise governments. "A jet plane with a
fringe on top," a friend called her.

As the best-known American, her trips abroad did much
to offset Soviet propaganda that the United States wished
to control other nations. Once when she was in France,
the Government there asked her to broadcast in French
over the radio to its people. She made several broadcasts
and all of France listened. In her quiet and simple manner
she made complicated issues clear and her optimism about
the future of mankind brought a warm response. A French
politician said of her broadcasts, "Her voice has done more
to create good will for the United States in Western
Europe than any other American."

In 1952, when she made an around-the-world trip to
the free and neutral nations, Radio Moscow denounced
her as "a sworn enemy of peace and democracy." This was
assurance enough that the Communists feared her influence. She stopped at Beirut, Damascus, Amman, Jerusalem
and Tel Aviv, where she held conferences with government leaders about their problems and made swift trips
into the countryside to talk with local citizens. Then she
flew to Pakistan for a week and to India for a month. In

India, Prime Minister Nehru doted on her like a brother.
He had her address the Indian Parliament and opened all
doors in India to her. Everywhere the comment on her was,
"If she is a typical American then the United States must
be a wonderful country."

When she went to Japan in 1953, a Tokyo paper said,
"Mrs. Roosevelt represents the conscience of America."
She made a special trip to Hiroshima to talk to the people
who had experienced an atomic bombing. When her inter-
preter started to cry when translating the miserable personal stories, she quickly took his hand. "I can understand
well without further interpretation," she told him.

In 1957, Mrs. Roosevelt made two important trips. One
was to Salzburg, Austria, the other to the Soviet Union.
In a camp near Salzburg were 3,000 Hungarian refugees.
They had rebelled against their Communist Government
the year before. These were stranded people, who had
hoped to be taken into the United States when they fled
Hungary. With action slow, these freedom fighters had
gone on a hunger strike.

Eleanor Roosevelt came to their camp when they were
already three days without food. They had vowed to die of
hunger unless permitted to come to the United States. "I
have some advice for you," she told them frankly. "By
your strike you have brought your plight to the attention
of the United States Government. However," she warned
them as a stern but understanding mother, "if you want
to emigrate to the United States you must get back on a
normal diet. Otherwise you will not pass the physical
requirements." Her talk broke the hunger strike.

Her trip to the Soviet Union came in September, 1957.
She talked to that country's dictator, Nikita Khrushchev,
for almost three hours. It was probably the first time an
outsider had talked with him on a give-and-take basis. She
told him that Soviet policy was disrupting and endangering

the peace of the world. "The Soviet Union wishes to spread throughout the world not only through the use of soldiers but through other agents," she charged.

"Am I also an agent?" he asked.

"You may have been for all I know," she told him.

Mrs. Roosevelt is well into her seventies now. She has not slowed down her pace, but maintains an eighteen-hour day. She has an apartment in New York City and a weekend and holiday cottage in Hyde Park. The Roosevelt family home in Hyde Park is now a museum.

She spends several mornings a week working for the American Association for the United Nations, where she is chairman of the board of governors. The purpose of the AAUN is to build up public support for the United Nations. She has played a large part in creating the 175 chapters of the AAUN that exist across the country.

There are many other things to attend to besides the AAUN, where she works without pay. Thousands of letters pour in each week from people who want her help. She does what she can for them. Once when she was unable to help a stranger further than to write him a sympathetic reply, he wrote her again a few years later. Her letter had filled him with courage, he said. "From then on a great change within myself took place." He had gone on to success.

She makes from 50 to 100 lectures a year. For this she gets about $30,000 which she turns over to various charities. On short trips she rides railroad coaches. She travels air coach across the ocean, sitting up reading all night. When in New York City, she averages about 15 appointments a day. She wears a hearing aid in her glasses and her bright expressive eyes she has willed to the Eye Bank.

Generally, there is a luncheon meeting, where she is expected to speak. Afterward, she dictates her newspaper column. Sometimes there are afternoon teas, or radio or television broadcasts for her. Occasionally she makes records. For instance, she did *Peter and the Wolf* with both the Boston Symphony Orchestra and the Tokyo Symphony.

At her cottage in Hyde Park, which was once part of her Val-Kill furniture factory, she has many mementoes of her life. There are many pictures of Franklin. There is also a picture of a heavy-faced man with a bristling mustache to which she points proudly. "That's Uncle Ted." Her eyes light up. When it is cold in Hyde Park, she goes on her daily hike wearing the same tweed coat Franklin bought her in Scotland on their honeymoon, back in 1905.

At Val-Kill, Mrs. Roosevelt busies herself in the charity that is dearest to her heart. This is the Wiltwyck School across the Hudson River. Here are New York's "most deprived and damaged children for whom no other institutional care is available." These are little "lost" souls coming from the worst slums in New York. She is one of the school's largest contributors in its effort to reclaim boys who are far beyond the juvenile delinquency stage. In a quiet way the school has worked wonders with its boys. Its most famous reclaimed "lost" soul is Floyd Patterson, the world's heavyweight boxing champion.

She has the boys of Wiltwyck to her cottage for picnics. Once when her face was overheated from buttering hundreds of buns for the boys, she was asked why she took on this servant's role. "When the King and Queen of England were here I buttered their rolls. Why should I do less for the boys from Wiltwyck?"

As she goes about her work, it is obvious that the prediction made sixty-five years ago by Uncle Ted's wife has long since come true. The ugly duckling has indeed turned out to be a swan!